SHIFT

A
Transformational
Journey From
Playing Small to
Unapologetically
Thriving

Dr. Nicole Yeldell Butts

PUBLISHING

For information contact : ATG Publishing info@atgpublishing.com - http://www.atgpublishing.com

ISBN: 9781991123510

First Edition: August 2025

10 9 8 7 6 5 4 3 2 1

ADHD
PUBLISHING STANDARDS
—— LEVEL 1 ——

Contents

INTRODUCTION

THE STORY BEHIND SHIFT

I knew early on what I wanted to do—who I admired, and who I wanted to emulate. And I knew exactly why.

I wanted to be Oprah Winfrey. Or Barbara Walters.

They spent their days being curious—asking questions, learning about people, unpacking ideas, and uncovering stories. They brought the world into my living room, one intimate conversation at a time.

They spoke with everyone from astronauts to activists, war correspondents to warmongers, moms making ends meet to business moguls making headlines. World leaders, actors, teachers, factory workers, victims, and perpetrators. But what struck me wasn't just who they talked to—It was how they talked to them.

Oprah and Barbara found the humanity in everyone. They made people feel seen, heard, and understood.

With anthropologist-like curiosity, they didn't stop at surface-level answers. They dug deep. With deep empathy, they leaned-in, they listened. They asked profound questions. They sought to uncover the "why behind the what". And they told people's stories with integrity and accountability.

Their trailblazing careers in broadcast journalism lit the path for me. Following that light, I chose to study the field at Howard University's School of Communication, stepping fully into a dream I had carried since childhood.

I still remember walking into the Howard University television studio—young, enthusiastic, self-impressed, confident, and ready.

But instead of rising to the occasion, I shrank.

There, behind the news desk and in front of the camera, sat Fredricka Whitfield. She was a senior—poised, polished, magnetic. Tall and graceful, with a swan-like neck and elegant shoulders, her long, dark hair cascading perfectly down her back. She had presence. Command. And there was no question—Fredericka was going far.

And then there was me, just starting out.

I remember the moment with absolute clarity. I gasped. Then I froze. My self-assuredness vanished. I withered. I forgot why I was there. I stepped back instead of stepping forward.

And I told myself a story that would quietly shape my life for years: That I wasn't built for the spotlight.

I wasn't worthy of that coveted space in which Fredericka sat. As with any shrinkage story, I needed to tell myself a cover story. So, I convinced myself that a journalist's life would be too hard, too uncertain, too demanding. That the long hours and constant hustle would make it nearly impossible to have a normal life—to do things like start a family or enjoy a sense of stability. That all I really wanted was a simple, predictable, safe life. There may have been some truth in those things, but the foundational truth was this: I abandoned myself and told myself a story to cover it up.

At the time, I didn't realize I was abandoning myself, and I most certainly didn't realize I had invented a cover story to explain it away. This realization took almost three decades to reach my consciousness.

At the time and for years after, I thought I was being practical. Journalism was risky and uncertain. I wanted stability and a family. So, I decided, *I'll just become a teacher.* That would be stable, predictable, and safe.

Here's what I know now: whenever we hear ourselves say *"I'll just…"*—we're not strategizing. We're shrinking.

I didn't abandon myself because I lacked talent or desire. I abandoned myself because I forgot my Why. I forgot the reasons driving my dream to become a journalist. And without that Why, I had no center or scaffolding strong enough to hold under the weight of that moment's uncertainty.

I let fear rewire my vision.

I didn't fall. I didn't fail. I faded.

I abandoned my voice, my dream, and my deeper purpose in exchange for safety. I abandoned myself to insecurity. To self-doubt. To comparison. And it wouldn't be the last time.

That's the thing about self-abandonment: it's not always loud. It's usually a whisper. Sometimes, it sounds like reason. It dresses itself up as humility, maturity, even wisdom.

But underneath all that rationality, I was stepping away from who I had once dared to be.

I spent the next three decades succeeding in ways that looked impressive—but didn't always feel aligned. I made choices rooted in responsibility, practicality, and progress.

I achieved my way through three degrees, three careers, and countless professional certifications. I married (twice). Raised a child. Bought homes. Traveled. Checked all the boxes. I impressed people with the beautiful life I'd built.

And I am proud of that life.

But here's the paradox…

From the outside, my life looked ordered, ambitious, and successful.

But on the inside, I was quietly navigating a persistent tension between achievement and alignment.

I was the woman who looked successful on paper—but felt like something essential was missing. I wasn't quite hitting the mark. I pivoted often. Each pivot was successful but still didn't feel fully aligned.

Because I had built a life of visible accomplishment—and moved with what looked like clarity and confidence—people assumed I always knew what I was doing.

But privately, I had started to wonder: *If I'm doing all the "right" things… why doesn't it sit right in my soul?*

The success was real. But so was the dissonance. Somewhere deep within me, a quiet question had started to stir—not loud enough to disrupt my life, but steady enough to shift the energy.

I couldn't name it yet, but something inside me was asking for more than achievement.

It was asking for alignment.

I didn't change anything right away. I kept moving—strategically, gracefully, and with the quiet ache of wonder still humming beneath it all.

I rarely asked for advice. I kept my own counsel. I didn't often process out loud. I made decisions quietly, and by the time I shared them, they were already fully formed.

My life choices appeared thoughtful and strategic, even when they defied convention. I made bold moves that often-surprised others—but they usually worked out. I appeared steady. Unshakable. Charmed.

No one doubted my decisions—they trusted me, even if they didn't always understand.

My mother called me impetuous. My brother shrugged. My husband sighed, calculating the impact my pivot would have on our shared life. My son high-fived me—this was the only version of me he had ever known. My friends asked questions, knowing there was always a purpose behind my choices.

What none of them saw was the quiet internal process that happened before I spoke a word aloud. What looked like spontaneity was often months—even years—in the making.

Over time, I became curious about how others responded to my choices, and even more intrigued by the questions they asked.

"How do you always seem to know what you're doing?" "How do you make such aligned decisions?" "Why do things seem to work out for you?" "Don't you ever have regrets?"

Beneath every observation was an unspoken assumption: "You seem to live with direction. With intention. With peace—even when your choices don't make sense from the outside."

And the truth is, I do.
Not because my life has been easy—it hasn't.
Not because everything has gone according to plan—it definitely hasn't.
But because I've followed a deeply rooted internal process.

At first, I wasn't fully aware of it. But the questions from others kept coming, so I began asking them of myself.

How do I trust myself so deeply? What allows me to pivot with clarity when others freeze? Why don't I carry regrets?

And in a season of deep personal reflection—after multiple transitions, brave decisions, and tender reckonings—I began to trace the thread. The thread that connected the curious girl I was to the woman I'd become. That childhood instinct to ask, connect, and understand had never left me. So, the questions became mirrors.

I began investigating myself, my choices, my why. Like a journalist or anthropologist of my own becoming, I dug beneath the surface.

And the reflection staring back revealed the framework I had been living all along. I wasn't making decisions based on others' expectations or some external script. I was making the best choices I could with the resources I had, grounded in my values and guided by the vision of the woman I was striving to become.

What began as a response to fear eventually became a framework for transformation. And it was that lived, personal process that I would one day recognize—and name—as SHIFT.

When I finally traced the pattern, I discovered a five-part process I had been following for years—a process that helped me navigate change with intention, courage, and clarity.

It helped me feel anchored even in chaos. It explained why people trusted my decisions—even when they didn't understand them. And why, even in the hardest seasons, I still felt intentional, strategic, purposeful, and whole.

At first, I didn't name it.
I didn't map it for others.
I wasn't creating a book or building a brand.
I was simply trying to understand myself.
That process is now the SHIFT framework.

It wasn't invented in a boardroom or a strategy session. It was excavated from real life—from shrinking and rising again. From reconnecting to my why. From aligning with my truth, not just my titles.

SHIFT is how I moved from success to significance. From reaction to alignment. From shrinking to becoming.

And the more I wrote, the clearer it became: SHIFT wasn't just mine. It was meant to be shared.

This book is the roadmap I followed—but never had.

It's the process that helped me stop shrinking, start shining, and stand fully in who I am.

And now, it's yours too.

YOUR INVITATION TO TRANSFORMATION

I didn't write this book because I have all the answers. I wrote it because I've lived the questions—and I know I'm not the only one.

I wrote it for the woman whose life looks successful on paper but doesn't sit right in her soul.

For the high achiever who keeps reaching milestones but quietly wonders, *Am I still on the right path?*

For the woman who's led the teams, raised the family, managed the expectations, and made it all look effortless—but inside, something is shifting.

I wrote it for the woman who has spent so long being strong for others and is finally ready to be true to herself.

I wrote it for you—if you've ever reached a moment were staying the same is no longer an option.

This book is not about perfection. It's about alignment. It's about consciously closing the gap between who you have been and who you want to become. It's for anyone ready to stop drifting and start deciding.

If you're anything like me—or like so many of the women that I coach and walk alongside—this book didn't land in your hands by accident.

Maybe something inside you is stirring. A quiet restlessness. A whisper reminding you that while your life may look "right" from the outside, something within is calling for more.

Maybe you've started asking the deeper questions. Or maybe you haven't said them aloud yet—but you've felt them in your body, in your spirit, in those still moments between responsibilities.

Or maybe you're at a crossroads—personally, professionally, or spiritually—sensing that something needs to shift, even if you can't yet name what or why.

And you don't have to be falling apart for change to be necessary or desired. Sometimes, transformation begins right in the middle of your success.

Right when the outside says you've made it—and the inside says you're just beginning.

This book is your invitation—not to become someone else, but to return to yourself. To the version of you that you may have buried under fear, responsibility, achievement, perfectionism, or self-sacrifice. The version of you that is powerful, worthy, whole, and ready.

If that's you, welcome. You're in the right place.

I hope this book meets you with equal parts compassion and challenge. I hope it holds a mirror to your truth and a map to your becoming. I hope it reminds you that transformation is not only possible—it's yours to claim.

You don't have to figure it all out today. You don't have to do it perfectly. But you do have to show up for yourself.

My hope is that you will not simply read this book, but use it. Use this book however you need. Read it from start to finish or linger in the chapters that resonate. Pause. Reflect. Journal. Revisit. Reread. Let the SHIFT framework meet you where you are and guide you where you're called to go.

This is your time. Your permission. Your turning point.

Wherever you are—uncertain, evolving, longing— consider this your invitation to begin.

If you are willing to be both conscious and courageous, you will not only change your circumstances, you will also transform your relationship with yourself.

Because here's what I know:
When women shrink, the world gets smaller.
When we remember who we are—and choose to become her fully—the world shifts.

CONSCIOUSNESS + COURAGE = TRANSFORMATION

True transformation doesn't begin with a strategy. It begins with a choice. A decision to wake up to your life. To stop drifting, stop shrinking, stop performing, and start becoming.

That choice requires two things: **Consciousness** and **courage**.

Without both of these, change remains surface-level. Temporary. But with both, something deeper happens.

You don't just shift your circumstances. You shift yourself. **Consciousness** is more than awareness. It's an awakening.

It's the moment you pause and begin paying attention—not just to what's happening around you, but to what's happening within you.

It's the willingness to examine how and why you make the decisions you do.

The willingness to trace the stories you've been telling yourself about who you are, what you're worth, and what's possible for you.

The willingness to notice your patterns. To question your fears. To challenge the beliefs that you inherited but never examined. To get curious about your motivators, your resistance, your desires, and the barriers you've internalized as truth.

When you become conscious of your internal landscape, you begin to see your life with new clarity. You recognize what's driving you—and what's holding you back. You reclaim the power to choose differently.

But awareness alone isn't enough. That's where courage comes in. **Courage** is what moves you from knowing to doing. From longing to becoming. It's not the absence of fear—it's the decision to move anyway.

Courage says:
Yes, this may be hard.

Yes, I might feel uncertain.
No, I don't have it all figured out.
But still—I will take the step.

Transformation is the result of having and practicing both consciousness and courage.

It's when you see your life clearly and dare to change it. When you honor your truth and move in its direction.

Consciousness sets the course. Courage fuels the journey.

When you walk with both, you don't just change your life—you reclaim it.

That is what this book will help you do.

Using this book as your guide, you will gain the tools to become both more conscious and more courageous. You will learn to recognize your own patterns, examine the stories that have shaped your choices, and reconnect with the version of you who has been quietly waiting to rise.

This isn't a blueprint for perfection. It's a framework for truth. A path back to yourself. A way to act with intention and integrity, to become the woman you were always meant to be—not just in your achievements, but in your alignment.

Bring your full presence and your whole heart to these pages. You won't just read about transformation. You will live it.

That is the promise of this journey. That is the power of SHIFT.

THE SHIFT FRAMEWORK

WHAT MAKES SHIFT UNIQUE

SHIFT is a five-point framework for intentional, conscious, courageous transformation.

It is a proven, repeatable process designed to spark meaningful breakthroughs, shifting not only how we think and feel but also how we show up and engage with the world around us. By consciously and courageously moving through these five steps, we begin to change our mindset, choices, and behaviors—while also reshaping the structural conditions in which we live, work, and relate.

To make this kind of transformation possible, the framework is built to be both personal and practical: comprehensive enough to go deep, clear enough to take action, and strong enough to sustain real change.

COMPREHENSIVE

Our lives are made-up of complex, integrated systems in which everything is interconnected and interdependent. Personal transformation requires a holistic approach that involves multiple aspects of our lives. SHIFT integrates five key dimensions: Purpose, Beliefs, Behaviors, Emotions, and Structures. Each of these aspects is interconnected, and neglecting any of them can undermine the success of the transformation.

Purpose is the compass of transformation. It is the first and recurring question of the SHIFT framework: *Why?*

Without a compelling "Why", transformation is neither relevant nor sustainable. Transformation without purpose is like setting out on a journey without a destination. It may be full of activity, but it lacks direction. A clearly defined purpose—our "Why"—anchors us when the journey becomes uncomfortable or uncertain. It gives meaning to the discomfort and clarity to our next step, even when the full path is not yet visible.

This "Why" is more than motivation—it is our internal North Star. It's the reason we begin the process and the fuel that keeps us moving. It may be a vision of the future, a longing for alignment, a desire to heal, or a call to expand. Whatever it is, it must be rooted in personal truth—not performance, pressure, or someone else's expectations.

In the SHIFT framework, purpose is not a one-time declaration—it's a recurring inquiry. Our "Why" may evolve as we evolve. What begins as a desire to feel more fulfilled might deepen into a calling to live more authentically. What starts as a professional goal might unfold into a personal reckoning. The clarity of our purpose determines the sustainability of our change.

To transform intentionally, we must keep asking: *What am I truly reaching for? What matters most now? And am I still living in alignment with my "Why"?* When our purpose is rooted in personal truth—not external validation—it becomes the fuel that carries us forward long after motivation fades.

Beliefs are the hidden architecture of our lives. They shape how we see ourselves, what we believe we deserve, and what we believe is possible. They operate in the background, influencing our choices, behaviors, and reactions—often without our conscious awareness.

Transformation requires surfacing and interrogating those beliefs. *Which ones align with our purpose? Which are inherited, outdated, or rooted in fear? Do we believe we are worthy of what we say we want? Do we believe change is truly possible for us— not just for everyone else?*

Transformation requires not only changing behaviors but shifting the beliefs that fuel them. When our beliefs are in conflict with our purpose, we'll unconsciously sabotage our progress. But when our beliefs are aligned with our "Why", we become unstoppable.

Rewriting limiting beliefs into liberating ones is both a mindset shift and a spiritual act. It means reclaiming authorship over our inner narrative and rewriting it in our own voice.

Behaviors are the actions and decisions we want to change or cultivate. What do we want to be different as a result of our "Why"?

Behaviors are where transformation becomes visible. They are the daily expressions of our inner work—what we say, what we choose, how we respond, and how we show up. Our behaviors are the evidence of our beliefs and the reflection of our values in motion.

To shift meaningfully, we must identify which behaviors support our vision and which ones sabotage it. *What patterns no longer serve us? What habits keep pulling us back into old versions of ourselves? Which actions feel aligned, empowering, and true?*

Change doesn't happen all at once. It happens in the micro decisions we make every day. The SHIFT framework helps move intention to action by creating behavior-based accountability and tracking what's working in real time. When we intentionally shape our behaviors to reflect our purpose and beliefs, we begin to embody our transformation, not just imagine it.

Emotions are always present. We cannot underestimate the impact of our emotions on our choices. Whether we acknowledge them or not, emotions are always in the room, quietly coloring our perceptions, shaping our decisions, and steering our behavior. Fear, shame, joy, desire, grief, hope—these are not side notes to change; they are the emotional undercurrents that determine how and whether we change.

Emotions are not distractions from transformation—they are doorways into it. Every decision we make is emotionally informed, whether we realize it or not.

Ignoring our emotions will sabotage our shift. But when we learn to recognize, name, and work with them, our emotions become guides, not obstacles. The key is to move from emotional reactivity to emotional intelligence—to get curious instead of critical when emotions arise.

What emotions are fueling our behaviors? What feelings emerge when we get close to change? What emotions are we trying to avoid, and how are they running the show?

Transformation invites emotional honesty. It requires us to sit with discomfort, grieve what we're releasing, embrace the vulnerability that comes with growth, and to honor joy. When we make space for our full emotional range, we free ourselves to transform from the inside out.

Systems & Structures are the routines, relationships, physical spaces, environments, habits, time, energy, and even what we physically, mentally, emotionally, and spiritually consume. Transformation doesn't happen in a vacuum. It is either supported or sabotaged by the systems and structures that shape our daily experience.

The question becomes: *Is my life designed to support who I am becoming—or who I used to be?*

If we're trying to shift while still living inside outdated systems, we will constantly encounter resistance. That resistance isn't always internal—it's also structural. We may have done the inner work, but if our surroundings, our schedule, or our relationships are still rooted in our past self, they'll pull us back like gravity.

That's why intentional restructuring is essential. Transformation often requires examining and redesigning the structures of our lives. This includes our physical environment, our social circles, our digital inputs, our habits, and our rhythms. *What boundaries need to be clarified or reinforced? What needs to be removed, added, or redesigned to help us sustain this change?*

We also have to ask: *How will I sustain this shift? What new practices, routines, and support systems must be put in place to keep me aligned and thriving?*

Without this layer of examination, transformation can remain surface-level—energizing but unsustainable. But when we intentionally align our structures with our purpose and our beliefs, we create the conditions for lasting change.

Transformation becomes sustainable when our life is built to support it. This includes not only practical strategies, but emotional scaffolding—community, accountability, and spaces that allow us to breathe, replenish, and grow. Systems don't just hold habits— they hold possibilities. When built with intention, they become a sanctuary for our becoming.

EFFECTIVE

Personal transformation often falters when there is no clear vision, no motivating tension between where we are and where we want to be, and no concrete steps to bridge the gap. It also stalls when we fail to address barriers such as deeply ingrained beliefs, unexamined habits, and structural or societal constraints. SHIFT makes transformation possible by aligning vision with strategy and intentionally recognizing and planning for barriers.

Aligning action with our vision is crucial for transformation because it ensures that our daily decisions are in sync with the desired shift. This alignment provides clarity and direction. Without this connection, even the most compelling vision can feel disconnected from reality, leading to change not taking place or being sustained. SHIFT ensures a vision is set, and all strategies flow from that vision.

Recognizing and planning for barriers is a critical part of the transformation process, which always involves uncertainty and risk. Without recognizing and planning for barriers and obstacles, transformational efforts can falter when unexpected challenges arise. SHIFT requires recognizing and planning for barriers early in the process.

MEASURABLE

When transformation lacks clear measures, it quickly becomes vague and directionless. Without something to track, it's hard to know what's working, what's not, or whether any real change is happening at all. Momentum stalls, motivation fades, and even meaningful efforts can feel like they're going nowhere.

That's why measurement matters. It gives us a way to see progress, celebrate wins, and adjust as we grow. It keeps us accountable to the vision and energized by it.

SHIFT weaves measurement and celebration into every step of the journey, making transformation not only possible but sustainable.

SUSTAINABLE

We've all seen it happen: a burst of motivation, a bold new habit, a promising change—only to watch it fade weeks or months later. Without reinforcement, even the most powerful transformation can slip back into old patterns.

Sustainable change doesn't happen by accident. It lasts when it's intentionally integrated into how we think, decide, and act—day after day. For transformation to endure, it must be effective, measurable, and consistently reinforced until it becomes part of who we are.

That's why SHIFT is built not just for breakthroughs—but for staying power. It's a framework for lasting change—because once something is truly transformed, it can never return to what it was before.

THE SHIFT TRANSFORMATIONAL JOURNEY

While the SHIFT Framework was excavated from real-life experiences, the journey ahead is yours. In the pages that follow, you'll step into your own journey of transformation, guided by the five steps of the framework.

Transformation is a journey, moving you from one point to another. It is not a journey that will happen quickly, and it rarely happens without intention.

As I explained in the Introduction, transformation requires both consciousness and courage to achieve. The awareness to know where you want to be, where you are now, and what it takes to close the gap, paired with the courage to take those steps.

It is often easier to just stay where you are, maintaining the status quo. But it takes courage to embark on a journey of transformation. This five-point framework will help you gain the consciousness and courage needed for the journey ahead.

This journey begins with a sense of purpose that guides you through unknown territories and new experiences. Along the way, there will be moments of challenge, discovery, growth, and reflection. Obstacles will arise, requiring resilience and adaptability, but each step offers opportunities. Ultimately, the journey shapes not just where you end up, but who you become along the way.

So, let's take a look at what makes up the SHIFT framework.

S: Set Your North Star

Because transformation begins with a clear vision and a compelling purpose that defines who you want to become, the first step in SHIFT is to Set Your North Star. The purpose of a North Star is to serve as a guiding point, offering direction and clarity as you move through your transformation. It is the fixed point you orient yourself toward. It is the clear, unwavering goal or vision upon which you stay focused, aligned, and purposeful even amid challenges or distractions. It anchors decision-making, ensures consistency, and inspires action by offering a long-term, meaningful target to strive toward. The next chapter will guide you through the development of a well-articulated vision that will serve as your North Star, providing direction and motivation throughout the transformational journey.

H: Here – You Are Here

Once you know where you are trying to go – your North Star – you need to figure out where you are currently, in relation to that North Star. Think of this step as the map you find at an amusement park or mall. There is a great big X that marks the spot where you stand. You can see where you are in relation to where you want to be. Chapter 3 will walk you through how to assess your Here, and will generate the creative tension needed to close the gap between your North Star and your Here.

I: Illustrate Your Path Forward

How exactly do you get from your Here to your desired there? With these two points established, in Chapter 4, you will chart a course for closing the gap between your current location and your North Star. You will determine high-impact areas of focus, and also determine short-term and long-term goals, objectives, strategies, and tactics needed to reach your North Star. You will plan for both barriers and enablers of success. You will establish ways to measure and monitor progress and celebrate wins.

F: Forge Ahead

With your Path Forward illustrated, in Chapter 5 you will Forge Ahead and begin the work you planned in the previous chapter. Most people start their change work at this step. They just jump right in, doing things without first setting their North Star, assessing where they are in relation to that North Star, identifying the gap between the two, and developing a detailed plan to close that gap. They just go right to activity. Again, one of the things that makes this framework effective is that it focuses on outcomes and results, not activity. This chapter is about putting into action all the work you have planned for up to this point.

T: Thrive Unapologetically

And finally, in Chapter 6, after Setting Your North Star, determining your Here, Illustrating Your Path Forward, and boldly Forging Ahead, you've arrived at a powerful moment in your transformation. You're either reaching for your vision, standing in the reality you once only imagined, or awakening to the truth that you've already become her. This chapter is about soaking it in. It's your invitation to own your growth, honor your journey, and fully embody the life you've been creating.

You don't have to be fearless or have it all figured out to begin. You just have to be willing. Willing to tell yourself the truth. Willing to do something different. Willing to choose yourself. As you move into the first step—Setting Your North Star—you'll begin by naming the vision that will guide you, the purpose that will ground you, and the truth that will carry you forward.

Let's begin.

FOLLOW MY JOURNEY

As you move through each step of the SHIFT framework, I'll be walking alongside you—sharing moments from my own transformational path. These personal reflections aren't meant to be instructions or ideals. They're real-life glimpses into how I've navigated this process: imperfectly, courageously, and with deep intention.

My hope is that by opening my journey to you, it helps you feel less alone in yours. That it gives you permission to reflect honestly, act boldly, and reclaim your own path—step by step, shift by shift.

In 2021, I SHIFTed my life. Ten years earlier–which turned out to be the circumstance of my second self-abandonment–I had married for the second time. My only child had graduated from high school and gone away to college. I moved back to Los Angeles, where I had grown up, and got married.

My first marriage failed for a multitude of reasons, but primarily because we simply didn't know how to be married, and for my part, I was impatient and entitled. In my first marriage, I did not change my last name; I hyphenated it. In 1993, when I did that, I thought it showed that I was independent, my own person, modern, and understood that marriage was just an add-on, not a change or replacement. Years later, as we were going through the divorce, and I very quickly dropped the hyphen and resumed using only my maiden name (mind you, before the divorce was even final), I realized that some of the decision to hyphenate also represented my lack of full commitment to the marriage. This is absolutely not true for everyone, but this is my journey and my reflections. In my mind at that time, my hyphenated name represented that I was not all in.

I was determined to go into my second marriage full throttle. I was older, more mature, and knew what I wanted. It was a second marriage for both of us, so we assumed we knew what we were doing this time around. I went in putting my marriage first. I dropped my maiden name and changed my last name to his last name. Proof that I was all in. I even spent the first several years thinking of our marriage as its own entity. It was not Brian. It was not Nicole. It was our marriage, and the marriage came first. At the time, that seemed healthy to me. Writing it now, the inevitable downfall should have been obvious.

When people talk about women losing themselves in their marriages or to motherhood, this is how it begins. But let me be clear: I didn't lose myself to my marriage. I abandoned myself to my marriage. I dropped Nicole off on the doorstep and hoped this unknown, still forming entity—our marriage—would take good care of her. But I was feisty and demanding, and he was stubborn and unbothered, so our marriage quickly became a war zone. But if we were nothing else, we were committed. Remember, this was round two for both of us, so we were determined to stick it out.

And we have. Fourteen years as I write this. But in doing so, I needed to take myself back. I could no longer abandon myself. The signs of self-abandonment had started to show up. I had gained weight. My hair had thinned. I was thriving professionally but felt personally and professionally stagnant. The dreams and goals I had held for myself had disappeared behind dreams and goals I had for this entity I called Marriage. I had put it first for so long that I had neglected my own dreams, goals, and ambitions.

*So, by 2021, I had a great deal of work to do to reclaim myself. And in typical fashion, I went full-out gladiator. I rented a lovely studio apartment in Arrowhead, California. I packed my car with groceries, candles, yoga mat, journal, computer, and art supplies. I drove through a historic snowstorm, up the mountain, and into the woods. I spent four days over the winter solstice laying out steps one through three of the SHIFT framework – **Setting my North Star**, **determining my Here,** and **Illustrating my Path Forward**.*

SET YOUR NORTH STAR

Transformation begins with a clear vision and a compelling purpose—a North Star that defines who you are intentionally becoming. In this step, you will develop a well-articulated vision that serves as your North Star. This North Star will provide direction and motivation throughout the transformational journey.

To become the person you want to be, you must first have a clear vision or picture of who you want to be. To become, you must first envision.

According to Dr. Stephen Covey in his book *The 7 Habits of Highly Effective People*, "All things are created twice — first in the mind, then in the real world." Physical creations follow mental ones. Just as homes are built according to blueprints, our lives are constructed from internal visions. To make your deepest desires a reality, you first need to see and understand what those desires are.

To "begin with the end in mind," as Covey suggests, is based on intentionality—the intention in your mind to create what may not yet be seen or actualized. To "begin with the end in mind" is to hold a vision of your future self before you begin pursuing it.

When you start with the end in mind, you're choosing a destination—your North Star. *Who do you want to be? How do you want to show up in the world?* Your answers to these questions become your North Star. That's why your SHIFT journey begins by defining it—so you can move forward with clarity and purpose.

THE NORTH STAR

Much like a navigator uses the North Star to chart their course, your North Star will act as a compass for your transformational journey—helping you set your course and continually assessing whether you're still on the right trajectory, or if adjustments are needed.

Without this guiding light, you risk becoming becalmed—stagnant, aimless, and adrift without a clear sense of movement or progress. The North Star helps prevent you from becoming lost or immobilized, offering a steady sense of purpose and inspiration. Without it, you may find yourself wandering in the dark, unsure of where you're headed and lacking a clear plan or markers to guide you. In its absence, navigating challenges becomes more difficult, and forward movement gives way to confusion, hesitation, and a loss of direction in the face of the journey's inevitable roadblocks.

Having a North Star allows you to:

Define a Clear Goal: Envisioning your desired result from the outset establishes a clear goal that acts as your destination. This gives you a fixed point to work toward, reducing uncertainty and providing clarity. A clear goal serves as your North Star, ensuring that all efforts are directed toward a meaningful, long-term objective.

Create a Roadmap: Once you know where you're headed, you can reverse engineer the necessary steps to get there. This helps in crafting a concrete plan of action with milestones aligned to your ultimate goal. A clear destination encourages proactive, strategic thinking, prompting intentional and long-term planning rather than reactive decision-making.

Stay Focused: With the end goal in mind, you can concentrate your energy on what matters most. This focus reduces distractions and prevents you from drifting in unproductive directions. It helps you make informed decisions, set personal boundaries, and determine what to prioritize or eliminate from your life.

Align Your Actions: When you know your destination, your daily actions and decisions can be aligned with your long-term goals. This alignment ensures that you stay on track and move consistently toward your vision. Every step becomes purposeful, reinforcing your commitment to your overall direction.

Adapt to Challenges: Challenges and obstacles are inevitable, but a clear end goal helps navigate and make necessary course corrections without losing sight of your destination. This clarity enables you to stay flexible while maintaining focus on your destination.

With your sights on your North Star, you can move forward with purpose, making every step meaningful and aligned with the larger vision. So how do you create a North Star?

To set your North Star, you must:

- Identify your values
- Explore what gets in the way of your values
- Decide how you will demonstrate your values
- Define and document your North Star

SETTING YOUR NORTH STAR

"You have to know who you are, and you live that reality. And you keep living it out no matter what."
Michelle Obama

A North Star begins with values. Values are the core beliefs that shape behaviors and actions, forming the foundation of how we live our lives. While we all have values—the things we say and believe are important—they don't always guide our behaviors.

Our stated values are the things we think we stand for. They represent who we want to be. Our values should determine our priorities and guide our behaviors, decisions, and actions. But they don't always.

Often, there's a gap between the values we believe we hold and the ones we actually live by—consciously or not. In other words, we may have stated values but not guiding values. When this happens, our behaviors are not fully aligned with what we claim to believe in.

Setting your North Star helps bridge the gap between the values you aspire to and the ones you actually live by—turning stated ideals into guiding principles that activity shape your decisions and actions.

In order to bridge this gap, you will need to first understand what your true values are and why they matter to you. Without this clarity, it's easy to unknowingly violate your principles. By identifying and consciously choosing your values, you can create a roadmap for living in alignment with them, allowing your North Star to guide you with purpose and intention.

When you are clear on your values, you are better equipped to persist through difficulties, act with assertiveness, and minimize regrets. In challenging times, your values will provide motivation and meaning, helping you focus on what's truly important. They will strengthen your ability to stand firm in the face of opposition and simplify decision-making by grounding you in what matters most. When you know your choices reflect your deepest values, you experience less self-doubt, less second-guessing, and greater confidence even in the toughest circumstances.

Consciously identifying your values is foundational to setting your North Star and transforming your life. Your values define the qualities you strive for and influence the way you show up in the world. When you choose them with intention, your North Star becomes more than just a destination—it becomes a reflection of who you are and who you are becoming.

Transformation begins with conscious intention, and it's your values that align your personal compass toward lasting change.

IDENTIFY YOUR VALUES

You must begin by identifying your values. Fair warning—this requires deep self-reflection. This means you must ask yourself—not others—questions about yourself. Ask, explore, and reflect on five key questions.

FIRST QUESTION: WHAT ARE MY VALUES?

Now, this first question probably sounds pretty easy. Trust me, it's not! Remember, I said this requires some deep reflection, so if it feels easy, you're probably not digging deep enough. If you think you already know the answer and simply jot down the first things that pop into your head—your standard list of values—three things are likely to happen:

1st: Your responses will be vague and overly broad. It might sound something like, "I value friendship" or "I value hard work." It has no real meaning, and it is not definitively actionable, which takes us to the second thing.

2nd: You'll think you've done something—but you haven't. You might feel confident that you know who you are and what matters to you. You may even feel a sense of pride or self-righteousness. But that feeling of accomplishment or moral superiority can become a block, keeping you from doing the real work of transformation.

3rd: You'll miss the opportunity to explore and examine the what, why, and how of your values. And that's where the transformational work really begins.

So, pause and truly sit with the question. Let it marinate. Let it resonate. As we discussed earlier, most people have stated values that are aspirational but not always lived. In order to turn your aspirational values into your lived values, you must be willing to spend time here. Don't rush. Clarity comes through stillness, not speed.

A value for me is human connection. I define connection as being able to see, hear and understand one another. I may not agree with someone's opinion, position, or actions, but it is important for me that I at least see that person as a person, hear them out, and try to understand the place from which they are coming.

SECOND QUESTION: WHY IS THIS A VALUE OF MINE?

Once you have identified those values, you need to understand why they are important to you. Transformation depends on the *why*. The *why* creates the purpose and the meaning which is needed for you to truly connect with your values. The *why* fuels the intrinsic motivation and ignites the passion. The *why* sustains the long-term commitment by promoting perseverance and enabling resilience. If you clearly understand your *why* you will be better positioned to reach your North Star.

"When your Why is big enough, you will find your how."
Les Brown

To uncover why those values are important for you, utilize the 3 Whys technique.

THE 3 WHYS

The 3 Whys is a modification of the 5 Whys technique, which is an interrogative technique used to explore the cause-and-effect relationships underlying a particular issue. The primary goal of the technique is to determine the root cause by repeating the question "Why?" Each answer forms the basis of the next question. Using my earlier example that I value human connection, the 3 Whys technique, for me, sounds like this:

1. Why is human connection important to me?
   Human connection is important to me because seeing another person is how we value each individual's humanity.

2. Why is valuing each person's humanity important to me?
   Valuing each person's humanity is important to me because if we don't value someone else's humanity, we

diminish their sheer existence.

3. Why is not diminishing someone's existence important to
    me?
    Because if I diminish one person's existence, I diminish the
    value of life.

It's through this deeper self-reflection utilizing the 3 Whys technique, that moves us past general statements like "I value friendship" and begins to uncover what those values truly mean in practice.

Now that I have used the 3 Whys to dig deeper into understanding why human connection is important to me, it will be much easier to live this value and much harder to ignore it when it is inconvenient. Why? Because for me, not making a connection diminishes the overall value of life. My value has a better chance of becoming a guiding value when I understand the whys behind it.

The Emotional Inflection Point

Transformation requires us to connect to emotion. If your main *why* is purely intellectual, the likelihood of making and sustaining a transformation is low.

Whenever you want to change something in your life — big or small, positive or negative, professional or personal — you start with something in your brain called the Intellectual Inflection Point. This is where your brain says, "I should stop smoking. I know it is not good for me." These intellectual reasons often don't hold. We fall back into the same habits. It is when we reach what is called the Emotional Inflection Point that change happens. For example: "I should stop smoking so I can see my grandchildren grow up."

Emotion is key to change. It is only when an emotional response is triggered that change happens. The emotional inflection point is a point on a curve where it suddenly and dramatically changes course. It is a point that results in extraordinary change. In determining the *why* behind your values, ensure that the *why* has an emotional aspect.

THIRD QUESTION: WHAT OBSTACLES GET IN THE WAY OF ME LIVING MY VALUES?

Values are foundational to setting your North Star, but obstacles can sometimes feel more powerful and compelling than the values we hold. While identifying your values and understanding the why behind them is essential, stopping there leaves you unprepared for the inevitable challenges that arise when trying to live them.

"If you fail to plan, you are planning to fail."
Benjamin Franklin

Obstacles are not dead ends—they are hurdles to be anticipated and navigated. If you don't acknowledge and prepare for them, they can hijack your journey, leaving you feeling uncertain, paralyzed, and off-course. Just as you've clarified your values, it's equally important to identify the obstacles you're likely to face when trying to live them. Only then can you stay aligned with your North Star.

To fully prepare for transformation, you must proactively anticipate what could get in your way. Failing to do so risks derailing your commitment to living your values. Remember, consciousness plus courage equals transformation. Consciousness is knowing your values and understanding how to demonstrate them. Courage is what allows you to face and overcome the challenges that try to pull you out of alignment.

By identifying and planning for these challenges in advance, you give yourself the power to act with intention and resilience. You won't be caught off guard—you'll be ready with a strategy. So, take time now to anticipate the obstacles that could interfere with living your values and decide how you'll navigate them when they arise.

There are two types of obstacles you'll face on your journey: internal and external. You'll likely encounter both, but which specific obstacles you encounter will depend on your chosen values and your personal circumstances.

Use the list below to reflect on common internal and external obstacles and begin identifying the ones most likely to show up for you.

INTERNAL OBSTACLES

Fear of Judgment or Rejection: Worrying about how others will perceive you can lead to compromising your values to fit in or avoid conflict.

Self-Doubt: A lack of confidence in your abilities or decisions can make it hard to stand firm in your values, especially when facing pressure from others.

Inconsistent Self-Awareness: If you're not fully aware of your values, or they are not clearly defined, it can be challenging to make choices that align with them.

Cognitive Dissonance: When actions and values are misaligned, this internal conflict can lead to discomfort or rationalizing behavior that contradicts one's values.

Habits and Conditioning: Deep-rooted habits or societal conditioning can create patterns of behavior that are difficult to change, even when they conflict with personal values.

Fear of Failure or Uncertainty: The uncertainty of the consequences of living by one's values (such as career or relationship risks) can make it difficult to fully commit to them.

Lack of Emotional Regulation: Intense emotions such as anger, frustration, or anxiety can cloud judgment and cause reactive behaviors that go against personal values.

Competing Priorities: Sometimes external demands or urgent needs can take precedence, causing individuals to temporarily sideline their values in favor of short-term gains or relief.

EXTERNAL OBSTACLES

Cultural and Societal Norms: Societal expectations or cultural traditions can pressure individuals to conform, even when these norms contradict personal values.

Workplace Dynamics: In professional environments, the policies, company culture, or leadership decisions may not align with your values, making it difficult to uphold them without risking conflict or career progression.

Peer Pressure: Friends, family, or colleagues may push you to act in ways that contradict your values, either overtly or subtly through their expectations or behavior.

Economic Pressures: Financial concerns or economic instability can force people into decisions (e.g., job choices, lifestyle compromises) that go against their personal values in order to meet basic needs.

Lack of Support: Without a supportive network, it can be difficult to live according to your values. Friends or family who do not understand or respect your values can create friction or alienation.

Institutional Barriers: Legal systems, government policies, or educational institutions might impose restrictions or create environments that make it hard to practice certain values, such as equality or freedom of expression.

Time Constraints: Busy schedules, demanding careers, or familial responsibilities can limit the time or energy available to pursue activities or decisions that align with your values.

Environmental Factors: Geographical location, local politics, or the availability of resources (e.g., access to healthy food, nature, or certain opportunities) can restrict the ability to live in harmony with specific values, such as sustainability or health.

Conflicting Interests of Others: Living your values may sometimes conflict with the desires or interests of others—such as in relationships, parenting, or business partnerships—making compromise difficult.

Social Injustice or Inequality: Larger societal issues like systemic inequality or discrimination may make it harder for some individuals to live out their values, particularly those related to justice, fairness, and equity.

Allow me to pause for a moment and point out a paradox. All external obstacles eventually become internal ones, because it's up to us how we choose to face and manage them. External obstacles do not emanate from us, but they are directed at us and ultimately processed by us. What we do with them becomes an internal decision.

This is where your North Star becomes essential. It keeps you aligned. It empowers you to make intentional choices. It helps you confidently define who you want to be, say yes to what matters, no to what doesn't, and establish healthy boundaries that honor your values.

FOURTH QUESTION: WHAT AM I GOING TO DO WHEN SOMETHING GETS IN THE WAY OF MY VALUES?

Once you have anticipated the obstacles, you need a plan for how you'll stay grounded when they inevitably arise.

Use the "When This, Then That" strategy to prepare specific responses, so when something threatens to pull you out of alignment, you already know how to respond in a way that honors your values.

When This, Then That

The When This, Then That strategy is a decision-making and problem-solving technique that links specific actions (the When) to particular responses (the Then). It's often used in behavioral psychology, personal productivity, and habit formation to create predictable outcomes based on situational cues. The key idea is to anticipate a trigger event ("When this happens") and pre-plan an appropriate action ("Then I will do that").

The strategy is simple but powerful, as it provides clear guidance on how to respond in specific situations, reducing uncertainty. It simplifies decision-making by removing the need to deliberate on responses during stressful or time-sensitive moments. It promotes habitual behavior by linking consistent responses to recurring triggers. And it encourages a sense of commitment by planning actions in advance, making it easier to follow through.

For example, one of my core values is human connection. A common obstacle arises in meetings when coworkers aren't seen or acknowledged. For instance, if someone talks over Mary and dismisses her dissenting view, I interject and say, "I'd like to hear what Mary has to say."

Without the "When This, Then That" strategy, I might just sit silently, feeling uncomfortable and out of alignment with myself. It could bother me for the rest of the day—not just because I feel bad for Mary, but because I'm disappointed in myself for not showing up as the person I want to be.

FIFTH QUESTION: HOW DO I WANT MY VALUES TO SHOW UP IN THE WORLD?

How do your values show up in the world? What do they look like, sound like, feel like? What do your values mean for the way you set priorities and make decisions? How do they shape the way you spend your money—and how you spend your time? How do they influence your interactions?

Simply having a list of values is not enough—they're just words until backed by action. While language gives voice to your values, it's your consistent, intentional behaviors that give them meaning. When your words and actions align, your values become a lived expression of what you stand for. When they don't, the dissonance erodes trust—both with others and within yourself.

Without clarity on how to demonstrate your values in the world, they remain abstract ideals, aspirational, rather than guiding principles. But when you know how to put them into practice, especially in moments of challenge or misalignment, your values become anchors. They ground your decisions in something real and help you stay aligned with who you truly are.

For each of your values, you must define the specific actions and behaviors that bring them to life. Revisit these questions as you do: *How does this value look, sound, and feel like in action? What does it mean for how I make decisions, or spend my time and money? How does it shape the way I show up and interact with others?*

And remember, you are setting your North Star. You are not describing your current behavior but rather envisioning who you want to be. These actions and behaviors may not be true of you yet, and that's okay. Don't limit your vision to your present reality. Think big. Aim high. Ask yourself: *What would it look like to fully embody this value? What decisions and behaviors would reflect the person I aspire to be? How do I want to show up in the world, and what will that require of me?*

DEFINE AND DOCUMENT YOUR NORTH STAR

You are now equipped with all the information you need to define and document your North Star. You have determined your values. You know why those are your values. You feel an emotional connection to your values. You have anticipated and planned the navigation of obstacles to those values. And you know how you want those values to show up in the world. Now you need to capture that all in one place for accessible reference.

Think of defining your North Star as being and doing. Your values are who you want to be. The demonstration is how you behave based on this. I want to be this person, and these are the things I will do to demonstrate being that person.

Write a paragraph defining your North Star. Use the first-person present tense. Your definition should include one Being sentence and several Doing sentences. Depending on the values and how divergent they may be, you might want to consider a paragraph for each one. Here is my example:

> *I am a person who values human connection. With curiosity and empathy, I engage in conversations with people who are different from me. I listen to understand the life experiences of others. In meetings, I provide space for everyone to share their perspectives.*

The first sentence: I am a person who values human connection is my Being sentence. The sentences that follow are my Doing sentences, as they describe the way I will demonstrate my being.

Using this definition, document your North Star in a way that feels most impactful, memorable, and actionable to you. It could be an image, a phrase, or a story—whatever makes your North Star meaningful and tangible. Remember: to be it, you must be able to see it.

Your North Star is not who you are today. It is who you want to become. Setting your North Star is the first step in the journey of transformation. Your North Star directs your journey. It is where you are navigating to. In order to chart a course, we need two points. Your North Star is where you are going. Your second point is where you are now. In the next chapter, you will assess where you are now. With those two points, your North Star and your You Are Here point, you will be able to illustrate your Path Forward in Chapter 4.

An Example of Creating Your NORTH STAR

Below is an example of the North Star exercise examining what I value, why I value it, what gets in the way, how I demonstrate it, and the final statement.

WHAT I VALUE & WHY I VALUE IT

Value: Exploration

Why do I value exploration? *I value exploration because I believe there is always something new to learn or experience.*

Why do I value new learnings? *I value new learnings because they keep my mind open to the world and the people in it.*

Why do I value my mind being open to the world and the people in it? *I value my mind being open to the world and its people because I want to live my life to the fullest.*

Why do I value living my life to the fullest? *I value living my life to the fullest because I only get one life.*

Why do I value only getting one life? *I value only getting one life because I don't know if or what comes after, and I want to get the most possible out of the one I have.*

WHAT GETS IN THE WAY

-competing priorities like work and making money.

-conflicting interest of others, like them not being as exploratory and/or not wanting me to expose them to my exploration.

HOW I DEMONSTRATE WHAT I VALUE

How do I demonstrate it: deep conversations, courageous conversations, reading, school, wandering, travel, living abroad.

MY NORTH STAR STATEMENT

(Being statement) I am an explorer.

(Doing statements) I engage in deep conversations to explore people's perspectives and ideas. I ask probing questions. I strike up conversations with people. I actively seek and engage in both formal and informal lifelong learning. I travel the world. I wander down unfamiliar roads. I metaphorically, and occasionally physically, dig deeper.

ANCHOR POINT

By the end of this step, you should have a clear picture of your North Star. To support and represent this, you should come away with a well-defined statement of who you want to become and how you will demonstrate that identity in your daily life. Your North Star is not just an abstract concept—it is a tangible, intentional guide that directs your choices, actions, and mindset. It is both your destination and your compass, keeping you aligned with your deepest values and aspirations, even when obstacles arise.

Through this process, you have explored the values that define you, uncovered the motivations behind them, and identified potential roadblocks that could divert you from living in alignment with them. You have also developed concrete ways to embody your values through intentional actions, ensuring that your North Star is not just a vision but a lived reality.

As you move forward, remember that transformation is not instantaneous—it is an ongoing journey of growth, self-discovery, and course correction. Your North Star will serve as your anchor, reminding you of who you are becoming and guiding you toward the life you want to lead.

In the next chapter, you will take the next critical step: Assessing where you are now.

Transformation requires both a clear vision of your destination and an honest understanding of your current starting point. With these two coordinates—your North Star and your present reality—you will be equipped to chart the path forward, ensuring that every step you take is intentional, aligned, and purposeful.

Your journey has begun. Keep your North Star in sight, trust in your vision, and move forward with confidence.

FOLLOW MY JOURNEY

In the winter of 2021, I created a 3-year vision statement for myself. It was my North Star. I gave myself 3 years to achieve this vision. It was chock-full of stuff! It included EVERYTHING. School, work, money, marriage, social, community, family, my house, my body, hair, and skin, my wardrobe, spirituality, philanthropy – EVERYTHING!

I started with my values. Those have always been pretty clear for me, but what I really needed to reconnect with was my Why and my How. Why were these particular values so important to me, and how was I demonstrating them? I did not know that valuing myself required just as much commitment as valuing my family. I thought in valuing my family and my marriage, I was valuing myself. But not when I was placing one above the other.

When I reflected on the question: "How do I demonstrate my value of self?" I came up empty. There was nothing I had been doing to demonstrate that I mattered. I had given it all away. This realization made me feel nauseous. I could not believe this intelligent, independent, self-sufficient, self-reliant, grown-ass woman was doing nothing to demonstrate her value to herself. WTF!

When I reflected on the question: "What gets in the way of demonstrating my value of self?" there was another bombshell. None of it was external. None of it. It wasn't even external pressure from my husband. It was all internal. I had completely and utterly done this to myself. My biggest obstacles were fear of rejection, fear of failure, and lack of emotional regulation. I was afraid of a second failed marriage. The failure of my first marriage I could explain away based on age, but my second marriage would not be so easy to dismiss. I was afraid that if showing up as a wife was not my first priority, my husband would reject me, and my second marriage would fail like my first one did. My emotions were all over the place. Anger, frustration, disappointment.

Armed with all this clarity and direction, I was able to set my North Star. And set it I did. That North Star was thorough, clear, and shining bright! It was—and continues to be—my guiding light and what I set my compass to every day. It keeps me on course. It helps me set my priorities and make decisions. It is my reminder when I feel myself slipping off course, abandoning myself.

HERE - YOU ARE HERE

In Step 1, you **Set your North Star**—the vision of where you want to go. And since you've begun this journey of transformation, it's safe to assume you're not there yet. That's why Step 2 of the framework is to identify where you are now—your **Here**.

Much like a mall or amusement park map, you can't chart a path to where you are going without first finding the **"Here - You Are Here"** marker.

These two points—your **North Star** and your **Here**—are like coordinates on a map. One marks your destination, the other your starting point. With both in view, you can move forward with clarity, intention, and direction.

So why is determining your **Here** step two and not step one? This is because we often start with our negatives and shortcomings. We often carry around a list in our heads and hearts of what we aren't doing right or should be doing better. We catalog all our flaws, faults, and failures. Let's just refer to this as our F³ List. This list tends to span every conceivable area of our lives, and it is neither helpful nor productive.

Examining our F³ list is not the objective of determining your **Here**. The objective of this step in the transformational process is to determine where we are in relation to our North Star. And not everything in our F³ list is relevant to our North Star. In fact, most aren't. To reach our North Star, we need to know where we are in relation to it so we can navigate our way from our Here to our there.

Determining your North Star first ensures that what you assess in this second step is purposeful, targeted, and aligned with your desired outcomes. For this reason, the SHIFT framework first has you determine your **North Star**, and then you assess your **Here**. Who do I want to be? How do I want to behave? My being and doing? That is what we will set out to assess.

Benefits of knowing your North Star before assessing your HERE	Problems with assessing your Here before determining your North Star
Focused and Relevant Data Collection: Defining goals ensures that the assessment targets the	**Uncertainty about what to assess/Lack of Focus:** Without clarity on what to assess, personal

most relevant areas, allowing you to gather data directly tied to your objectives. This helps avoid wasting time and resources on irrelevant information.

resources – time, energy, money, emotion – can be wasted on gathering and making sense of irrelevant information or analyzing areas that do not contribute to reaching your North Star. Without a clear target, assessing lacks direction, making it difficult to determine what information is relevant, important, and supportive of goals. You could end up analyzing areas that aren't aligned with your North Star, wasting resources on irrelevant information, and becoming misled by things that are not important.

Clarity in Decision-Making: When you know what you aim to achieve, the assessment process becomes clearer and more purposeful. This clarity ensures that the results provide actionable insights directly aligned with your strategic goals, aiding in more effective decision-making.

Overload of Information: Assessments can generate a lot of data, but without goals to narrow the focus, it becomes difficult to sift through and make actionable decisions. Too much data without a guiding purpose can cause decision paralysis or create red herrings, having you go down roads you don't need to go down.

CREATIVE TENSION

Of all the benefits of developing your North Star before assessing your current state, the greatest is its ability to generate creative tension. **Creative tension** comes from seeing clearly where we want to be, in this case our North Star, and being clear about where we are—our current reality. Creative tension refers to the gap between a person's current reality and their desired vision. This dynamic tension is considered "creative" because it drives motivation to close the gap and achieve the desired outcome.

To harness creative tension effectively, it's important to understand what makes it work. Here are the key components:

Current Reality vs. Vision: Creative tension arises when there's a clear awareness of the difference between the present state (current reality) and the future state (desired vision or goal). Recognizing this gap is essential for motivating change and improvement.

Energy for Change: The tension between where you are and where you want to be, creates a driving force or energy that pushes you toward action. This can inspire new ideas, strategies, or solutions that bridge the gap.

Proactive Problem-Solving: Creative tension encourages a mindset of innovation, as you are forced to think about how to overcome challenges and obstacles that stand between your current state and your goals.

Sustained Focus and Commitment: By keeping the vision clear and constantly comparing it to the current reality, creative tension helps maintain focus and commitment to the goal. It provides a reminder of why change is necessary and what needs to be done.

Healthy Discomfort: Unlike stress caused by negative pressure, creative tension is a constructive form of discomfort. It pushes you to stretch your capabilities, explore new approaches, and move beyond complacency or inertia.

Without vision, there is no creative tension. Creative tension cannot be generated from current reality alone. The drive to change reality comes from holding a vision of what could be—one that matters more to you than what is. In essence, creative tension fuels growth and progression by harnessing the energy of the gap between what is and what could be.

Steps 1 and 2 of the SHIFT Framework—completed in that order—allow you to generate creative tension.

DETERMINING YOUR HERE

"Your big opportunity may be right where you are now."
Napoleon Hill

To fully understand your Here, you will:

- Gather information
- Analyze and prioritize information
- Drop a pin at Here
- Review and reflect

GATHER INFORMATION

You don't know what you don't know. Without honest assessment, you might assume you're closer to, or farther from, your North Star than you truly are. That's why you need to assess where you are now, so you can plot it clearly. When you identify both your Here and your NorthStar, you gain the clarity needed to chart your course and begin closing the gap.

To determine where you are, you need accurate, meaningful insights—and those come from multiple sources. There are three primary places to gather information to assess your Here: yourself, your surroundings, and input from others. Each source plays a critical role in shaping the clarity, relevance, and impact of your assessment.

Self-Assess

When conducting a self-assessment, asking thoughtful, reflective questions is essential for gaining meaningful insights. Brutal honesty is key. The more transparent you are with yourself, the more clearly you'll understand your current state. And the clearer you are about your Here, the better you can chart a course toward your North Star.

Focus your self-assessment on the values and behaviors that align with your North Star. The goal s to identify gaps between who you are now and who you are striving to become. To do this, critically examine your past decisions and actions. Where have they reflected your core values? Where have they strayed from your vision for your life? This reflection will reveal where realignment is needed and where you're already on track.

ASSESS INCONSISTENCIES

Are there areas where your behaviors or decisions frequently conflict with your stated values? For example, if you value work-life balance, are you frequently overworking or neglecting personal time? If you value respect, do you sometimes interrupt others or fail to listen actively?

LOOK BACK AT KEY MOMENTS

Reflect on significant decisions or actions over the past few months or years.

Ask yourself:

- *Did my decisions reflect my values, or did I compromise them?*
- *Were there moments when I acted against my values? Why?*
- *How did I feel after making decisions that were aligned (or misaligned) with my values?*

For example, if integrity is a value, consider how often you were transparent and honest in challenging situations.

REFLECT ON SPECIFIC SITUATIONS WHERE YOUR VALUES WERE TESTED

Looking closely at moments when your values were challenged helps you assess how you respond in a real-world context. *How did you respond when faced with an ethical dilemma at work? When under pressure, did you act in ways that reflected patience, empathy, or integrity? Did you make decisions that advanced your ambition but conflicted with your commitment to collaboration or service?*

Analyzing these situations can reveal whether your behaviors align with your values or where there's room for greater alignment.

CHECK YOUR SURROUNDINGS

Your surroundings—physical, social, or professional—serve as mirrors, reflecting how closely you're living in alignment with your values. They offer important cues and feedback that can deepen your self-awareness and help you assess how well your behaviors and environment support your values and goals.

To gather information about your surroundings, consider the following:

PHYSICAL SPACE

Analyze whether your physical environment reflects your values. Look at your workspace, home, or any other environment where you spend time. *Do they reflect your values and priorities?*

For example, If you value organization and productivity, is your workspace tidy and conducive to focus? If you value creativity, do your surroundings inspire you with art, books, or other elements that spark innovation? Notice how your surroundings affect your energy and mood. Are you comfortable, focused, and energized, or do you feel distracted and stressed? Your environment can affect your behavior, so assess whether it supports or hinders your goals.

PROFESSIONAL ENVIRONMENT

Analyze whether your professional environment reflects your values.

Ask yourself:

- *Do the organization(s) I work for, or with, reflect my values and priorities?*

- *Does the work I do reflect my values and priorities?*
- *Does how I work align with my values and behaviors?*
- *Am I working at a level consistent with my values?*

SOCIAL ENVIRONMENT

Your social environment acts as a mirror, continuously reflecting how aligned you are with your values. The people you choose to surround yourself with—friends, family, colleagues—don't just influence your decisions; they often reveal your current level of self-awareness and personal integrity.

Ask yourself:

- *Are the people in my life aligned with my values?*
- *Do people in my life pull me away from my values?*
- *Do I have anyone in my life who shares my values? If so, who?*
- *Do I have any mentors, and if so, who?*
- *Who do I admire in my social or professional environment? Why do I admire them?*

Understanding which values or behaviors you appreciate in others can help clarify whether you are living up to them.

COMMUNITY ENGAGEMENT

Your community, both in-person and online, is a stage where your values play out in real time. The communities you are a part of—whether professional networks, volunteer groups, or social circles—

can give you clues about how aligned you are with your values. For example, if you value service, but you are not engaged in community or philanthropic activities, you may notice a gap between your stated values and your behavior.

Being part of a vibrant, supportive community reinforces values like collaboration and mutual respect, which can help you assess how well you embody these values in interactions with others. Consider your presence in digital spaces, too.

Ask yourself:

- *What communities am I currently part of—professionally, socially, spiritually, or civically?*
- *What do my online profiles and interactions say about my values and behaviors?*
- *Am I projecting the person I want to be?*
- *Do my online actions align with the image I have of myself?*

INTAKE

What you consume—books, media, conversations, content—is shaping you, moment by moment. Intake isn't just entertainment or information; its nourishment (or noise) for your mind, heart, and identity. Just as we are mindful of what we feed our bodies, we must be intentional about what we feed our inner world.

Ask yourself:

- *What am I reading, watching, listening to, and scrolling*

through?
- *Do these things reflect my values?*
- *Do they support the person I want to be?*
- *Will they support my journey?*

What you take in becomes part of your internal ecosystem. They have a significant influence on our thinking, perspective, emotions, decisions, and how we relate to others. They feed into how we perceive and interact with the world.

FEEDBACK FROM ROUTINE ACTIVITIES

Analyze whether your daily habits and routines reflect your values. Your daily routines—how you spend your time, energy, and attention—offer insights into your values. For example, if you value health but consistently skip exercise or neglect self-care, this might indicate a disconnect between your stated values and your actions. If you value learning but aren't investing time in reading or developing new skills, that might be an area to assess and improve.

Ask yourself:
- Do my routines reflect my values?
- Do my routines drain my energy or energize me?
- Do my routines support my goals?

ASK FOR INPUT

Critical for gathering information on your Here is seeking input from people around you. Soliciting feedback from others is a crucial part of understanding how your values and behaviors show up, and how well they align with the way you want to live and work. Since others often see us from different perspectives, their input can reveal blind spots, highlight strengths, and offer valuable insights into how consistent we are in demonstrating our values. Consider the following to effectively gather input from others:

CHOOSE THE RIGHT PEOPLE

Select people who interact with you regularly and whose opinions you trust. These individuals should be able to provide honest, constructive feedback without fear of causing discomfort. Aim for a mix of people from different areas of your life—work, personal, social—to provide well-rounded feedback.

For example, colleagues or peers can give input on how you act in professional environments, leadership, or collaboration. Supervisors or mentors may offer insights on your behavior in high-stakes situations and whether you live your values under pressure. Friends or family can offer perspective on your personal life, values, and how you balance personal and professional responsibilities.

BE CLEAR ABOUT WHAT YOU'RE ASKING FOR

Stay focused on your North Star. When asking others for input, share your core values, and be clear that it is these values and corresponding behaviors you want them to provide input on.

For example, ask them, *"I value integrity, and transparency ...*

- *"How well do you think I demonstrate these values in our work together?"*
- *"Do you see my actions and behaviors reflecting these values?*
- *"Can you provide examples where I demonstrated or failed to demonstrate these values?"*

Encourage feedback with specific examples of actions or decisions that reflect—or fail to reflect—your values. This makes the feedback direct, relevant, and actionable. Emphasize that you are seeking honest input to support your growth, and that you welcome both affirmation and constructive critique. Make it clear you are not just looking for praise, but that you are inviting insight into where your behaviors may not align with your values.

Encourage them to reflect on both strengths and any inconsistencies they've observed. Balanced feedback will help you identify blind spots, validate progress, and surface opportunities for deeper alignment.

ASK OPEN-ENDED QUESTIONS
Invite thoughtful, reflective responses that go beyond simple yes/no answers. Open-ended questions allow for deeper insight and help surface patterns you might not see on your own.

Examples include:

- *"Can you describe a time when you saw me living one of my core values? What stood out to you?"*
- *"Is there an area where you think I could do a better job of aligning my actions with my stated values?"*
- *"How do you think my behavior impacts those around me, particularly in terms of the values I say I hold?"*
- *"Where do you see me struggling to live out my values?"*
- *"What specific behaviors do you think are inconsistent with the values I say are important to me?"*
- *"Is there an area where you think my values could be stronger or more clearly demonstrated?"*

Gathering information is not the end—it's the foundation. Now that you've taken an honest look at yourself, your environment, and how others experience you, it's time to make meaning of what you've discovered. Information alone doesn't create transformation. What matters is how you interpret it, what you learn from it, and how you choose to respond.

In the next step, you'll begin analyzing the insights you've collected, identifying patterns, and determining which areas are most important to address. This is where clarity begins to emerge— and where SHIFT starts to take shape.

ANALYZE & PRIORITIZE THE INFORMATION

Once you have gathered insights from the three primary sources—yourself, your surroundings, and others—it's time to analyze what you've learned. This step is essential for identifying growth opportunities and turning raw information into actionable insight. Effective analysis means synthesizing what you've collected, looking for patterns of alignment or misalignment, and identifying which areas should be prioritized for change. Here is how to approach the analysis.

ORGANIZE AND CATEGORIZE THE DATA

Sort the information you've gathered into meaningful categories aligned with your North Star. Group insights from your self-assessment, feedback from others, and observations from your surroundings into areas such as strengths, challenges, behaviors, and habits.

Identify areas where you feel there is a strong alignment with your values, as well as areas that need improvement. Look closely at how your surroundings either support or hinder your goals.

LOOK FOR PATTERNS AND TRENDS

Pay particular attention to recurring themes across your different sources. For example, if your self-assessment reveals a struggle with focus, and feedback from others has mentioned the same, this is a pattern worth exploring. Likewise, if both your surroundings and external feedback highlight collaboration as a strength, that may be a strength to leverage.

Look for discrepancies between your self-perception and how others perceive you. These gaps may highlight areas for growth. For instance, you may believe you communicate effectively, but if others mention experiencing confusion or miscommunication, that may indicate a disconnect to address. Conversely, others may recognize strengths in you that you've overlooked, which may signal untapped potential.

ANALYZE ALIGNMENT WITH VALUES AND GOALS

Compare the patterns you've identified to your North Star. *Where are you living in alignment with your values? Where are the gaps, inconsistencies, or areas of dissatisfaction?* Highlight the areas where you are doing well, and pinpoint where there are significant issues or dissatisfaction.

PRIORITIZE FOCUS AREAS

Your North Star identified key values and behaviors you want to demonstrate, and your information gathering and analysis revealed some truths about what you're currently displaying, and how. Before you move forward, you will need to prioritize an appropriate and reasonable number of key areas to focus your attention on. To allow for an effective, measurable, and sustainable transformation, I recommend limiting your key areas to 3 to 5.

If there are multiple areas, focus on those with the greatest impact. Identify which gaps most significantly affect your ability to reach your North Star. Consider which areas, if left unchanged, most conflict with your North Star and pose the greatest risk to your sense of self, who you want to be, and how you want to show up in the world.

DROP A PIN HERE

DESCRIBE YOU'RE HERE

With this analysis, describe your current state. Paint a clear picture, using specific examples, of where you are right now. Like using a GPS, drop a pin to mark your location. Just as you defined your North Star, consider defining your Here in terms of both being and doing: Who are you currently being? What are you currently doing?

Write a paragraph in first-person present tense, describing your Here. Just like you did with your North Star, feel free to express your Here in a way that feels most impactful and memorable to you. If you're visual, represent it as an image or a color. If you're auditory, describe it as a sound. If you're rhythmic, let it take shape as a phrase, poem, or song. What matters most is that it is meaningful to you. Pin It. This is your Here.

PLOT THE GAP

You now have two points. You have your North Star, which tells you where you are going, and you have your Here which tells you where you are now. You have your starting point and your end point. You can now plot the gap—the distance—between the two.

You can create a textual or visual representation of the gap using whatever method is most understandable, meaningful, impactful, and memorable to you. As an example, here is a simple comparison chart to visualize where improvements are needed.

Key Area	North Star	HERE	Gap
Travel			
Collaboration			
Innovation			

Don't worry right now about filling in the steps to close the gap. You will do that in Step 3, Illustrate the Path Forward. All you need to do right now is create a way for you to see and understand the gap. This will help build the creative tension discussed earlier.

REVIEW & REFLECT

Knowing your Here is only part of the story, and with only part of the story, you don't have full understanding or meaning. Knowing where you are without knowing how you got here—or what is keeping you here—is only providing limited knowledge. You need a deeper understanding of the current state to effectively close the gap between your Here and your North Star.

If you were on a road trip and discovered you weren't where you thought you were, that knowledge wouldn't help you get to your destination—especially if you got lost by reading the map upside down, and you're still holding it that way. Similarly, revving the engine while stuck in the mud won't help if you don't realize that what's keeping you stuck is a lack of leverage.

In order to fully understand your Here, you need to reflect on two things: How you got here and what has kept you here.

HOW DID YOU GET HERE?

How did you get here? Some people spend years or decades in therapy trying to understand who they are and why they do what they do. This is not that! You are here to focus on your North Star, what has kept you from reaching it so far, and what you are going to do next to reach it. Your reflection is focused on this.

Your current Here is not an accident. It's the result of all the beliefs, assumptions, behaviors, practices, and decisions up to this point. If you want to transform, you must first understand how you got Here. That means considering:

Foundational Beliefs: Foundational beliefs are deeply ingrained assumptions or convictions about life, people, the world, and your place in it. These beliefs are often shaped by culture, upbringing, education, religion, and personal experiences. They operate at a subconscious level, forming the basis for the values you hold, the goals you set, and the decisions you make. *What are some of your foundational beliefs that brought you to your Here? How have these beliefs shaped your day-to-day behaviors and decision-making?*

Limiting Beliefs: Limiting beliefs are thoughts or convictions that restrict your abilities, choices, or opportunities. They can manifest in the form of "I can't," "I'm not good enough," or "It's not possible." They restrict your potential and create barriers to achieving your goals by reinforcing negative thoughts, self-doubt, or fear.

These beliefs usually stem from past experiences, societal conditioning, upbringing, or fear of failure. Many limiting beliefs operate at a subconscious level, influencing your thoughts and behaviors without you even realizing it. *What are some of your limiting beliefs that brought you to your Here? How have these beliefs shaped your day-to-day behaviors and decision-making?*

Rationalization: Rationalization is the process of justifying or explaining your behavior, decisions, or beliefs in a way that seems logical or reasonable, even if it does not align with your values. It often involves creating excuses or reasons to reconcile actions that contradict your values or to avoid discomfort or guilt.

I unwittingly used rationalization when I decided to be a teacher instead of a broadcast journalist.

When there's a conflict between what you do and what you believe (your values), cognitive dissonance arises. Rationalization is a defense mechanism that helps reduce this mental discomfort by justifying actions that go against your values. Be aware of when you may have rationalized behavior that goes against your values.

Conflicting or Contradicting Values: Sometimes you have conflicting or contradictory values that have gotten you Here. Conflicting or contradictory values occur when two or more values that are important to you are in opposition to each other, leading to tension, confusion, or difficulty in decision-making. Failure to identify and navigate this conflict can prevent you from acting in alignment with either value. *What may be some conflicting values to the ones laid out in your North Star?*

Storytelling: *What stories are you telling yourself about yourself that have gotten you Here?*

I value adventure and exploration—intellectual, spiritual, physical. But on a trip to Turkey, I found myself saying no to hot-air ballooning in Cappadocia. Why? Because I'd been telling myself for decades that I was afraid of heights. That long-held story had become part of my identity.

But after some intentional reprogramming, I rewrote the story I had been telling myself about myself. I decided I didn't want to be a person whose fear of heights would derail my deeper sense of adventure—especially while exploring the world. And then I soared over Cappadocia in a hot-air balloon. It wasn't just a ride. It was a reclaiming of my adventurous self.

What stories have you told yourself about yourself that have brought you to your current Here?

Patterns: What are some patterns that have gotten you Here? As I write this book, I am not in the physical condition I would like to be. My husband often reminds me that when it comes to exercise, I have a pattern of inconsistency. I go really hard for a few months, then I cease all activity for several months. My pattern is basically gladiator-sloth-gladiator-sloth. What are some of your patterns?

IDENTIFY WHAT IS KEEPING YOU HERE

"What we don't change, we choose."
Michelle Obama

We don't remain in situations that offer us nothing. Even if it's just the comfort of the familiar or protection from the fear of the unknown, we're getting something from where we are. The question is: what are you gaining by staying Here? And just as importantly, what's been holding you in place?

Reflecting on what keeps you in your current situation is important because it helps uncover the underlying forces—both internal and external—that may be influencing your choices, actions, or inaction. Understanding these forces enables you to make informed decisions and break free from patterns that may be limiting growth or progress. As Michelle Obama says, 'What we don't change, we choose.' This process is about gathering the information you need to choose something different.

Explore the forces that keep you Here. Yours will be unique to you, so I strongly encourage you to take the time needed to sincerely reflect on this question and uncover your holds—the things that are holding you Here. Below are some factors that may cause you to engage in behaviors that contradict your stated values.

Habits & Conditioning: Many behaviors become ingrained through habit. Even when you consciously know that a behavior is not aligned with your beliefs, breaking habitual patterns can be challenging. You may stick to familiar behaviors because they feel comfortable or because they've become your default—even when you know they're not ideal or no longer serving you.

Social Pressure & Expectations: Society may promote values or behaviors that conflict with your personal values and beliefs. At times, you might find yourself going along with them to fit in or to avoid judgment, rejection or conflict.

Fear of Consequences: You may fear the consequences of living fully in alignment with your beliefs. Fears like losing opportunities, making others uncomfortable, stepping into unfamiliar territory, or facing social exclusion may lead you to choose safety over authenticity.

Emotional Attachments: Sometimes, certain behaviors or choices offer emotional comfort or stability, even if they don't reflect your values. These attachments can make it hard to let go, even when you know you are not aligned.

Immediate Gratification: You may prioritize short-term ease, comfort, or reward over long-term goals and values. This can lead to choices that provide immediate satisfaction but conflict with your deeper beliefs.

External Rewards or Incentives: Sometimes external rewards—such as money, status, or power—can make it tempting to act against your values. The desire for these external incentives may override your commitment to your internal beliefs.

You may not always be fully aware of how your behaviors may contradict your beliefs. A lack of self-reflection or mindfulness can prevent you from recognizing the gap between what you believe and what you do. But when you ask yourself how you got Here—and what's keeping you Here—you bring unconscious patterns into conscious awareness. To make meaningful change, you must first be conscious of your reality. Only then can you be courageous enough to change it.

ANCHOR POINT

By completing this step, you now have a clear and honest understanding of your Here. You have defined where you currently stand in relation to your North Star, examined the internal and external influences that have shaped your current state, and reflected on the beliefs, habits, anc patterns that may have kept you Here. This self-awareness is critical—it provides the foundation upon which real transformation is built.

Understanding your Here is rot about judgment, but about clarity. It is not about dwelling on past mistakes, shortcomings of your F³ list; rather, it is about seeing yourself and your reality truthfully so that you can chart an intentional path forward. Without an accurate assessment of where you are, any attempt at transformation will lack direction and focus.

Now that you have two critical points—your North Star and your Here—you are equipped with the necessary perspective to navigate your transformation. The gap between these two points is not something to fear; it is an opportunity. It is the space in which growth, learning, and change happen. The tension between where you are and where you want to be creates the energy needed to propel you forward.

In the next step, Step 3: Illustrate Your Path Forward, you will begin mapping the journey between these two points. You will determine the key steps required to move from your current reality toward the future you are creating. You will identify the skills, behaviors, and mindset shifts needed to bridge the gap and set yourself up for sustainable transformation.

As you move forward, keep in mind: Transformation is not about perfection—it is about progress. Your Here is only temporary. The most important thing is that you now have the awareness, insight, and motivation to take action. The journey continues, and the next step will bring your vision to life in a tangible, actionable way.

Your transformation is already in motion. Keep going.

FOLLOW MY JOURNEY

Reflecting on my Here and doing a scan of my surroundings was startling and eye-opening.

Earlier in my life, I had never read a self-help book. They simply were not part of my reading repertoire. Yet, when I checked my surroundings, I realized I had dozens of marriage self-help books. DOZENS! Old and new. From stuff written in the 60s to stuff written yesterday. Written by men, by women, by couples. Faith-based; archetype; feminine energy; masculine energy. It made up my reading, my social media time, my internet research. It was all I was taking in. For fuck's sake!

I also realized that in the ten years I had been back in Los Angeles, my social group had expanded in an interesting way. The friends I had grown up with—my girls—were still my girls, and they would always be my girls! While my network of girlfriends expanded only slightly, the network of friends my husband and I shared as a couple had grown significantly. We were surrounded by other married couples. Which has its benefits, as it feeds me as a wife and us as a couple. But it did not feed me as an individual. For that, I still returned to the same small community of women I grew up with.

In terms of my physical surroundings, my home was entirely shared space. My husband had a man cave with a pool table and sports memorabilia, but it also had the largest TV, so we often watched television there together. I still maintained a bedroom for my adult son who lived across the country. In the end, the whole house felt shared. Other than my side of the closet, I had no dedicated space for myself. Why? Because I was sharing my life, and I had not carved out anything, not even a niche, for myself. I loved my house, but it was a communal space.

I had very little community engagement. I was not engaged with any church, civic organizations, or volunteerism. My daily routines felt stale, stagnant, and uninspiring, and seemed to drain me more than enliven me. Don't get me wrong. As a couple, we were very active and busy: Concerts, music festivals, dinner parties, world travel, homecoming games, weekends with friends. Our social calendar was full. Our passports were stamped. We were having fun, but I was depleted. I was feeding us, but I was not feeding me.

I looked at how I got here. I discovered that I had not so much a conflicting value but dueling values. I value family, and I thought that in valuing my family and my marriage, I was valuing myself. But not when I was placing one above the other. And because I had not been cognizant of these dueling values, I did not navigate them effectively. When I looked at what was keeping me Here, I had to separate out keeping me in the marriage or keeping me stuck in putting the marriage before myself. I decided it was not the marriage that was the problem, it was the way I was existing in the marriage that was the problem. That helped me realize I did not need to focus on what was keeping me in the marriage, I needed to focus on what was keeping me stuck in my abandonment of self. And the only thing that was keeping me there was a lack of awareness. Now that I was aware—conscious—I could and would make different decisions.

What I Got Wrong:

I was on fire! All this reflection and revelation set me up for an amazing North Star. As I mentioned, my North Star was ALL-ENCOMPASSING. What I did not do well was the part of the step when you prioritize the key high-impact focus areas. Yeah, I didn't do that part! I hit EVERY aspect of my life. I left nothing to chance and nothing out. And I gave myself a whole 3 years to achieve it. (If you did not read the sarcasm in my words, they are there. Go back and reread that last sentence in a sarcastic tone.)

I took it all on simultaneously. My kryptonite is thinking I can do it all. And I can. Just not at the exact same time. I was going to earn a doctorate degree, run a consulting business, work a full-time job, write books, do TED Talks, all while bodybuilding, being an attentive daughter, daughter-in-law, mother, sister, and friend. All of this while I was either jet-setting around the world or at home surrounded by candles, plants, and flowers—knowing damn well that I have killed every plant I have ever had. Trust me when I tell you there was more. Not the least bit realistic. But luckily, somewhere around the end of the first year, I realized my folly and gave myself a break.

My North Star has not changed. It remains the exact same. What has changed is the way I use it. I will say more about this in the next *step.*

ILLUSTRATE YOUR PATH FORWARD

"Goals are dreams with deadlines. Plans are the roads that get you there."
Diana Scharf Hunt

In Step 1, you Set Your North Star. In Step 2 you explored your Here. Now in Step 3, you will Illustrate Your Path Forward, closing the gap between your North Star and your Here.

When you know exactly where you stand and have a clear vision of where you want to end up, you're ready to start designing a path between the two.

In this step, to Illustrate Your Path Forward, you will:

- Create a detailed roadmap
- Identify and navigate hazards
- Identify and leverage havens
- Stay on course with mile markers, fueling stations, checkpoints, and scenic views

There can be a variety of ways to reach your North Star. Your Path Forward is wholly unique to you based on where you are now, where you want to go, and the path you choose to get there. No two journeys are the same. What is important is that you plan your journey. For example, varying paths to your goal of learning to play piano might look something like this:

Different Paths to the Same North Star		
1. Take extra shifts at work to save up money for a piano.	1. Sign up for a group class at the local community college.	1. Download a virtual piano program to your computer – something that offers interactive lessons, song libraries, and feedback features.
2. Buy a piano.	2. Attend classes.	
3. Hire a piano teacher.	3. Practice the songs assigned, starting with easy pieces such as "Ode to Joy".	
4. Practice the songs assigned, starting with easy pieces such as "Ode to Joy".		2. Start with the beginner-level tutorials included in the app.
5. Keep practicing and begin to	4. Keep practicing and begin to learn more intermediate	3. Begin practicing simple songs such as "Ode to Joy".

learn more intermediate pieces, like Billy Joel's "Piano Man". 6. Finally, ask your teacher to teach you "Fur Elise" by Beethoven. 7. Practice the piece until you've mastered it.	pieces like Billy Joel's "Piano Man". 5. Finally, ask your teacher to teach you "Fur Elise" by Beethoven. 6. Practice the piece until you've mastered it.	4. Begin learning more intermediate pieces like Billy Joel's "Piano Man" using the apps intermediate lessons. 5. Search for a digital tutorial for Beethoven's "Fur Elise". 6. Practice the piece until you've mastered it.

CREATE A DETAILED ROADMAP

In Step 2, Here, you identified 3 key high-impact focus areas of your transformation, and you plotted the gap between your Here and your North Star. I told you not to worry about filling in the steps to close the gap because we would do that in Step 3. This is where we are now.

Once you have prioritized your key high-impact focus areas, you will need to establish goals and illustrate how you will achieve those goals. For each area, illustrate a clear plan outlining how you will close the gap between the current state and your ideal state. How are you going to reach your North Star?

For each of your 3 high-impact focus areas, you will create a roadmap from your Here to your North Star. This will involve identifying the specific actions you need to take to arrive at your destination. When you look at your 2 plotted points from Step 2, what do you need to do to close the gap? This may include a variety of things. Some to consider are:

Thoughts & Storytelling: *What comes into your head? What thoughts do you need to reframe?* I am starting with thoughts and storytelling because all the other areas on this list ultimately stem from these. Your thoughts are the stories you tell yourself—about who you are, who others are, and what's happening around you. You are always telling yourself a story, always narrating. It is how people make meaning. But not every story you tell yourself is helpful.

Challenge the stories you tell yourself. The next time a thought or judgment enters your mind, pause and ask yourself:
- *"Is that true?"*
- *"Where did that come from?"*
- *"Why do I think that?"*

Challenge the narrative. Don't just accept the thought—interrogate it. Then, reframe it. When a limiting or unhelpful thought surfaces, consciously shift it to something more truthful, compassionate, or empowering. For example:
- Instead of *"I always mess this up,"* try *"I've struggled with*

this before, but I'm learning and improving."

- Instead of *"I'm not good enough,"* try *"I'm still growing— and I'm already enough."*
- Instead of *"This will never work,"* try *"This is unfamiliar, but I'm open to what's possible."*

Reframing isn't about pretending—it's about choosing a story that aligns with your growth, not your fear.

Knowledge: Knowledge is the foundation for transformation. It's the awareness, understanding, or familiarity you gain through learning or experience. It includes facts, concepts, insights, and context, all of which support growth. Ask yourself: *What knowledge do I need to reach my North Star?*

For example, one of my North Stars is: "I am a citizen of the world. I travel globally and reside in both the United States and Morocco." To move toward that vision, I need to understand Moroccan visa laws. *What types of visas are available? What are the eligibility requirements? Which one allows part-time residency?*

Skills: Skills are proficiencies you develop through learning, practice, and experience. These could include public speaking, leadership, or even language acquisition. Continuing with my North Star example, a skill I need to build is speaking Arabic or French. That will require commitment, practice, and new habits.

Behavior: Behavior includes your actions, reactions, and choices. For example, I've taken French and can understand more than I can speak. But when I have the opportunity to speak, I often don't because the story I tell myself is that I'll sound foolish. That thought creates avoidance. To reach my North Star, I need to shift that behavior and practice speaking when I have the chance.

Habits and routines: Our habits shape our outcomes. Some habits support our North Star, and others hold us back, especially when they're linked together. Years ago, I lost 20 pounds by limiting evening television. Why? Because when I watched TV, I snacked. I couldn't seem to do one without the other. So, I eliminated the TV habit, and the snacking stopped too.

What habits are linked in your life? What habit could you remove or build that could create a ripple effect? For me, walking early in the morning sets the tone for healthier choices all day.

Symbols & Artifacts: Degrees, certifications, and licenses are symbols of learning or accomplishment. They represent structured growth. But sometimes we wait for these markers before we allow ourselves to move forward. I did this with my doctorate, telling myself I needed the title before I could fully step into who I wanted to be. Sometimes we need the symbol. Sometimes we're just stalling.

Support Systems & Relationships: *Do you have the people you need* *around you to help you get to your North Star? If not, how can you build that support?* When I started my doctorate at age 50, I looked around for help—and realized I was already surrounded by friends with doctorate degrees. That support made the journey feel possible. Your environment can either lift you toward your vision or keep you tethered to where you've been.

Physical space: Your environment can help or hinder your progress. My sister meditates every day—and has created a dedicated space just for that practice. When I was writing this book, I needed a consistent space to write. Not every North Star requires physical space, but some do. My North Star of being an author does. My North Star of being a citizen of the world? That one's about mobility, not a specific space.

Community & Networks: Some journeys require community. You may need to find one—or create one. For instance, Black Girls Travel Too is a company dedicated to Black women travelers. A decade ago, finding travel companions was difficult. Now, I can sign up for one of their curated trips and be surrounded by like-minded women. That community started with a woman who couldn't find what she needed—so she built it.

Professional Environment: Sometimes your job needs to change. Sometimes your relationship with your job needs to change. At one point, I commuted 120 miles roundtrip every day. I couldn't even think about personal growth—I was just surviving the traffic. Even after that job ended, my professional life consumed more time than it deserved. I was successful by external standards, but I wasn't using my gifts in ways that aligned with who I wanted to become.

Create a chart with your North Star at the top and identify those things you need to do to close the gap between your Here and there.

I am an explorer. I live in Morocco part-time.	
Knowledge	What types of visas allow me to live in Morocco six months a year? What are the eligibility requirements? How do I apply? How long is the approval process?
Skill	Fluent in French
Behavior	Practice speaking French. Create a "Morocco" savings account.
Community	Join ex-pats in Morocco social network groups.

Another approach you can take is what I refer to as The Staircase. You build the staircase from the top down, and then follow it from the bottom up.

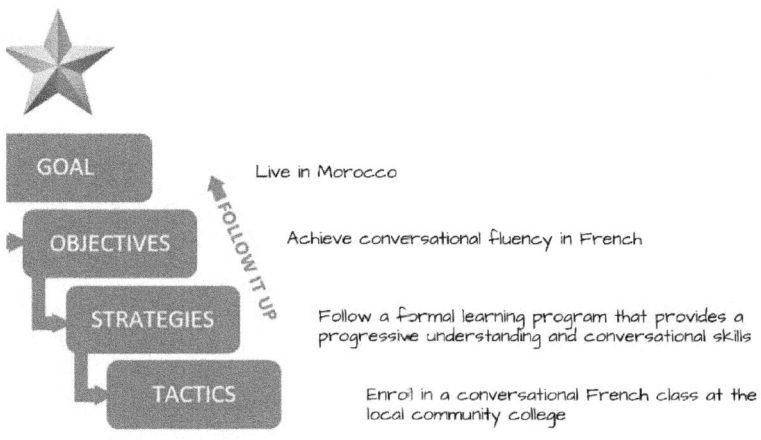

IDENTIFY & NAVIGATE HAZARDS

As you Illustrate Your Path Forward, remember—it's not enough to just plan what you need to close the gap; you also need to commit to the actions that will get you there. This includes preparing for hazards, things that will get in the way of your journey—roadblocks and detours. There are always hazards. To increase your chances of reaching your North Star, you must prepare for these in advance. Go into your journey anticipating what is going to get in your way, how you will recognize it, and how you will respond.

A roadblock is a barrier that prevents you from moving forward on your path. It represents obstacles that force you to stop, reconsider, or find a way around. Roadblocks can symbolize challenges that require problem-solving and resilience. Or they could require adapting your plans, finding alternative solutions, or seeking support.

Detours represent obstacles that don't stop you completely but force you to take an alternate, often longer route, to reach your destination. They symbolize delays, setbacks, or challenges that cause you to temporarily change direction but ultimately keep you moving forward.

Both roadblocks and detours signify the challenges and obstacles that disrupt progress, requiring adaptability, persistence, and creative problem-solving to continue the journey. Additionally, they offer new perspectives and valuable lessons along the way.

Some hazards will be personal or internal, and others will be external. Both are equally hazardous to your journey, so you need to determine before you set out how you are going to recognize and navigate them.

Think back to Step 2 where you identified the things that have gotten you to your current Here, and the things that have held you there. Some were internal and others were external. Those will likely be roadblocks and detours for your journey. Revisit those and consider the impact they may have on your roadmap.

Now that you have a roadmap, you'll likely encounter additional roadblocks and detours specific to the steps you've outlined. Look at the actions you have on your roadmap. *What internal and external obstacles can you anticipate?*

Internal Hazards		
Obstacle	How will I recognize it?	How will I navigate it?
Embarrassment	I will become nervous and shy when spoken to in French.	I will use my When This Then That strategy. When I feel embarrassed, I will remind myself that in order to have any level of independence when I move to Morocco, I must be able to communicate.
External Hazards		
Obstacle	How will I recognize it?	How will I navigate it?
Social pressure	I will notice friends or family questioning my decision, minimizing its importance, or encouraging me to stay.	I will remind myself that their resistance likely comes from love for me and fear for me. I'll revisit my North Star and reaffirm that this

		move is part of my intentional journey. I'll thank them for their concern but stay grounded in my purpose and the life I'm building.

IDENTIFY & LEVERAGE HAVENS

The good news is just as there are hazards along the way, there are also havens—straightaways and greenlights. *Havens* are your enablers. *Enablers* are factors that facilitate your path forward. They support, accelerate, or make change easier to implement. These elements create a conducive environment for change to take place and succeed.

Enablers are things you have in place that will serve you well. You want to identify them up front so you can leverage them for your success.

To uncover enablers, ask questions that help identify strengths, resources, and positive factors that could support your North Star. You want to be able to identify your own personal internal enablers and also the people, tools, and resources that could enable your success, as well. The following key questions may help you uncover them.

Internal Enablers

- *What strengths or skills do I already possess that will help me achieve my goals?*
- *What past successes can I reflect on to build confidence in my ability to achieve future goals?*
- *What processes or strategies have worked for me in the past that I can apply again?*
- *What resources (time, money, tools, support) are available to help me move forward?*
- *Are there any habits or routines that consistently help me stay productive and motivated?*

External Enablers

- *What external factors or opportunities can I leverage to my advantage?*
- *What key people (mentors, colleagues, friends) can support and guide me?*
- *Am I part of any networks or communities that provide opportunities, resources, or advice?*
- *What aspects of my work or living environment enable me to stay focused and on track?*
- *What systems or tools (technology, apps, etc.) help me stay organized and efficient?*
- *Are there external enablers (market trends, technology, timing) that can accelerate my success?*

- *Has someone else done something similar that I can use as a model?*

By recognizing enablers and barriers early, you can proactively address challenges, create a supportive environment for change, and increase the likelihood of a successful transformation.

STAY ON COURSE WITH MILE MARKERS, FUELING STATIONS, CHECKPOINTS & SCENIC VIEWS

Once you have your course set and your hazards and havens labeled, you must determine how you will track your progress and keep yourself motivated. Knowing that you are moving in the right direction is helpful for the journey. To support your journey and stay on course, you will need to plan for mile markers, refueling, checkpoints, and scenic views. Let's look at each of these.

Mile Markers: *How do you define and measure success? What are the mile markers on your journey?* Mile markers help you stay on track by making progress visible—showing how far you've come and how far you still have to go. Without them, the journey can feel endless and uncertain. Establishing clear mile markers allows you to monitor your growth, celebrate wins along the way, and stay motivated. Take time now to define what those markers will be for you.

Fueling or Charging Stations: *How do you keep your energy up on a journey?* You need fuel or a charge. Fueling and charging stations allow you to refill your tank or recharge your battery. You can put air in your tires, clean the windshield, throw out trash, stretch, and get a snack. They offer an opportunity to rest and recuperate so you can stay energized for the next phase of the journey. Failing to refuel or recharge will leave you stuck on the side of the road, unable to progress. So don't miss these stations. Plan them on your map. What exactly and specifically are you going to do to stay fueled and energized?

Checkpoints: *How do you hold yourself accountable?* Checkpoints are moments along your journey where you may pause to assess or evaluate. Much like a travel checkpoint might involve inspection or questioning, these moments offer an opportunity to reflect, review, and ensure you're still on course. A checkpoint represents accountability—whether to yourself or from others—and provides a structured space for updates, feedback, and honest self-assessment. It's a touchpoint to confirm you're taking meaningful action and remaining aligned with your goals.

Consider enlisting one or more accountability buddies—people who know your North Star or specific goals and are committed to helping you stay on track. You might have different accountability partners for different areas of your journey. Their role is to offer encouragement, feedback, and a sense of responsibility. Your role is to check in regularly, share updates, discuss challenges, celebrate wins, and outline next steps. They may help you problem-solve or simply serve as a supportive ear. Either way, they act as a meaningful point of accountability to keep you aligned and moving forward.

Scenic Views: Yes, reaching your destination is a reward—but if it's the only one, you're reducing your chances of getting there. To sustain motivation and prevent burnout, it's important to celebrate incremental progress with small rewards along the way. Think of these as scenic views on your journey—moments of enjoyment and reflection that remind you how far you've come and inspire you to keep going. These rewards reinforce your efforts, acknowledge your growth, and make the process more fulfilling.

ANCHOR POINT

At this stage in your SHIFT journey, you have Set your North Star, identified your Here, and Illustrated Your Path Forward. You now have a clear roadmap—one that is uniquely yours—guiding you from where you are today to where you want to be.

Your Path Forward is not just a plan; it is a commitment to action, transformation, and growth.

You have identified the key steps needed to close the gap, anticipated potential roadblocks and detours, and leveraged enablers to support your success. You have established mile markers to track your progress, fueling stations to keep you energized, checkpoints to hold yourself accountable, and scenic views to celebrate your wins along the way.

Now comes the most important step of all: Taking action. A beautifully drawn map is useless if you never take the first step. Transformation happens when you move—not when you wait, hesitate, or perfect your plans indefinitely.

As you move into Step 4: Forge Ahead, you will bring your roadmap to life. You will begin making the necessary shifts, taking deliberate action and actively closing the gap between your Here and your North Star. The journey is no longer theoretical—it is real, and it starts now.

You are prepared. You are ready. You have everything you need to begin. Forge Ahead with confidence, knowing that each step forward brings you closer to the life you are creating.

FOLLOW MY JOURNEY

In Step 1, I shared that my North Star was thorough, clear, and shining bright—and included EVERYTHING! It encompassed every aspect of my life. I also mentioned earlier that I tend to go full-out gladiator. Well, Illustrating my Path Forward was no different. I illustrated a Path Forward for EVERY aspect of my North Star. I do not say this with pride. I say this with a bit of embarrassment.

What I Got Right:
I thoroughly Illustrated my Path Forward. I identified my thoughts and storytelling, and I reframed those that were out of alignment with my North Star. I determined the knowledge and skills I needed to acquire, and the attitudes, behaviors, and routines I needed to eliminate, change, and adopt. I determined the symbols and artifacts I wanted to obtain. I determined the spaces I needed to be in and those I should not.

I called out my roadblocks and detours. I enlisted my enablers. I mapped out my mile markers, fueling stations, checkpoints, and scenic views.

My plan was so detailed and so clear that anyone who may have picked it up could have followed it.

What I Got Wrong:
I forgot the beauty and practicality of selecting only 3-5 focus areas to

prioritize. In Step 2, I asked you to prioritize focus areas. I wrote, "To allow for an effective, measurable and sustainable transformation, I recommend limiting your key areas to 3-5."

Full disclosure - this got added to the framework when I failed to do it. When I took on EVERYTHING all at ONCE and had to keep readjusting because I had not set reasonable limits in the first place. I realized that if I don't include a limit to key areas in the framework, others would make the same mistake I did. Beast Mode, although initially invigorating, was not sustainable. After lots of readjustments to the plan and timelines I had established, I had to realize that focusing on getting my doctorate degree was enough all by itself. The other things could – and did – wait.

INTERLUDE: A MOMENT OF REFLECTION

Before we continue, I want to take a moment to pause and reflect. In the introduction, I shared the phrase, "I make the best choices I can based on who I want to be and the information I have at the time."

Let's take a moment to unpack this.

Why pause to reflect on this phrase now? Because at this point in the SHIFT framework, you've done remarkable work. You've consciously and intentionally defined who you want to be by setting your North Star. You've gathered insight into who and where you are today, and made choices about beliefs, behaviors, and actions that align with your North Star. Before Forging Ahead, it's important to reflect on the concepts of grace and rejecting regret.

This interlude is about trusting your vision and your choices—granting yourself grace and choosing to live without regret.

"I make the best choices I can..."

When you make a decision, you're weighing the pros and cons, aiming to choose the pros you can live with and the cons you can tolerate. Some cons, however, are simply intolerable—those are often the source of regret. But by acknowledging what you can or cannot live with at the time of decision-making, you honor your choices.

"...based on who I want to be..."

You are making choices with a long-term vision in mind—a commitment to your values and to becoming your highest self. This person may not be exactly who you are today, but it is who you strive to become tomorrow. I am always striving to be the best version of myself. My decisions aren't based on remaining stagnant; they're motivated by a desire to evolve and improve. But this is not about dissatisfaction or an endless pursuit of perfection. I'm satisfied, even thrilled, with my life today, and I'm proud of my journey. Yet, as long as I'm alive, I will strive for growth. Your vision of your highest self is the compass that drives your decisions.

"...with the information I have at the time."

Regret is something I avoid because I trust that, given the information I had and the person I was at the time, I made the best choice available to me. I grant myself grace because I recognize that past decisions were made with my best effort, aligned with my vision and values. Could I make a different decision if faced with the same situation today? Maybe. In some cases, it's likely. But here's the key: The exact same situation cannot exist today because I am not the same person I was then. My life, my experiences, and my options are all different now. So why expend emotional, mental, or psychological energy trying to analyze past choices through the lens of time and space continuums?

As you Forge Ahead, do so trusting yourself, granting yourself grace and releasing regret. Know that you are making the best choices for yourself, based on who you want to be, with the information you have at the time.

FORGE AHEAD

"You have to practice who you want to be. You don't simply wake up one morning, and you're suddenly who you think you want to be. You have to put some energy into it. You have to practice it."
Michelle Obama

In Step 1, you started with the end in mind, defining who you want to be and Setting Your North Star. In Step 2, you determined where you currently are in relation to that North Star by identifying your Here. In Step 3, you designed a roadmap to close the gap between your North Star and your Here by Illustrating Your Path Forward. Now is time to Forge Ahead and implement your plan.

I mentioned in the Introduction that what makes the SHIFT framework unique is that it starts with the vision—the why before the what and the how. Most individuals, when looking to make a change in their lives, don't do that preliminary work. They just jump right in and start doing without first knowing why, what or how. That approach is reactive and impulsive, and usually ineffective. It is often driven by immediate emotions like anger, frustration, or fear. You know when this is happening. You can tell because there is a deep sense of urgency. There is usually some external force driving this need to action. It is always about the doing, never about the being or the why. I refer to it as Reactive Doing and it may sound like:

- I am going on a liquid diet. I need to be able to fit into this dress for the wedding next month.
- This sale is ending soon! I know it's not in the budget, but I'm buying it now before the sale ends.
- I'm done! I'm quitting even though I don't have another job or income lined up.

When you Forge Ahead without having Set your North Star, knowing your Here or Illustrating Your Path Forward to close the gap, one of the following is going to happen:

- You'll find yourself stuck in place, exerting effort without traction, unable to move forward despite how hard you push.
- Or, you'll loop endlessly without direction, covering ground but never making real progress.

In both cases, you're depleting your resources—time, emotional and mental energy, money, and even belief in yourself. Worse still, you're missing aligned opportunities because those resources are being spent on unproductive motion. And unlike gas, these are not resources you can easily refill. Once spent, they're often gone.

The good news is this does not have to be you. At this point, you have done the initial work needed to avoid Reactive Doing. Let's recap all the tools you have ready as you Forge Ahead.

You have your North Star. Who you want to be and, most importantly, why. Your why encompasses an emotional inflection point that will support your staying the course. Your North Star has aligned your Being with your Doing. In other words, you have identified the behaviors that demonstrate your values. You know the obstacles you may encounter, and you have a plan to navigate them.

You know where you are now. Where you are starting the journey. You know how you got to where you are and the things that have kept you where you are. You have plotted the two points and established a creative tension between your current state and your ideal future state.

You have illustrated a path forward. Prioritizing your key focus areas and crafting a roadmap to bridge the gap between your current state and your North Star. You know the goals, objectives, strategies, and tactics you need to enact. You know the tools that need to be developed. You have identified how to track and monitor progress, and have even forecast and planned for barriers and enablers.

You are now ready to proactively Forge Ahead and implement your plan. To do so, you will:

- Get ready to work
- Implement your Path Forward
- Refine your strategy
- Reflect on your journey

GETTING READY TO WORK

One of my favorite things to do is to get ready to work. I love planning and organizing before I get to doing. Sometimes this looks like preparing my desk. Or making sure my office is neat and orderly. The things I work with are close at hand. I can see those things that bring me joy as I work—my flowers and plants. To help you get ready to work, consider the resources you need to organize and any conversations you may want to have.

ALLOCATE RESOURCES

Allocating resources is a form of preparation and organization, and it is essential for ensuring you have the resources needed to reach your destination.

Time: I am starting with time as a resource, as this is the resource I see people most often neglect. If you are working through this framework, you have already put in quality time with planning. You must also allow time to do the work you planned for, as well as time to reflect on your journey. You'll need to make time in your day and week not only to follow through on what you said you'd do, but also to give yourself enough time to reach your destination. You won't reach your North Star next week or next month—and you're not supposed to. What you should be doing next week and next month is taking aligned action. You may hit a few important milestones over the next few weeks or months, but if you've already arrived at your North Star in that time then what you created likely wasn't a true North Star—it was just a to-do list.

Finances: Allocating the proper financial resources ensures that the transformation is adequately supported. Failing to allocate funds can lead to failure. Make sure to budget and plan. You may not have all the financial resources in hand at this moment, but again, you are on a journey. So plan for what is coming in the future and budget for it.

As important as planning is, it is also important to take actions in an appropriate order. When I was applying to the University of Southern California, my husband kept asking, "How are we going to pay for this new degree?" I didn't have that answer yet. But what I knew was that the answer to that question was not relevant if I did not get in. I first had to apply, hopefully be accepted, and then enroll. If I focused on not knowing how I was going to pay for it, or if I assumed I could never afford it, I would never have applied, and I would never have known.

Take actions in the appropriate order, and do not put the cart before the horse, as the old saying goes. Finances are typically not the what, they are part of the how. Take care of the why and the what first, and the how will take care of itself.

Experts: *Are there people who can help you reach your goals? Do you need to invest in coaches, trainers, marketers?* Depending on your North Star, you may need help from people who are experts in a particular field. When I was writing blogs, I needed to pay an editor to review my copy before I put it out there. As I was reassessing my wardrobe and what it said about me, I had to ask a friend whose style I admired to help me look at my closet differently. I liked dresses because I did not need to figure out what top went with what bottom. Dresses were like a one-pot meal for me—easy, fast, and did not require creativity. But I felt bored and uninspired by my attire and wanted to step it up a bit. She was a great resource. In Step 3: Illustrate Your Path Forward, she would also be considered an enabler. Someone in my circle I could use to help me meet my goals.

Physical Space: *Do you have the physical space you need to begin work?* My sister is also a writer. She found it helpful to utilize shared writing spaces. They were quiet but not isolated, they had beverages and snacks, technology, and a stimulating vibe. That kind of space served her purposes perfectly. I, on the other hand, am either writing at home in my now dedicated office space or holed up in a rented studio in the desert for a week, cranking it out. Does your physical space accommodate your needs?

Technology: *What technological tools do you need to support your journey? Do you already have access to them? If not, how can you acquire them?* Just like finances, don't let a lack of access stop you from moving forward. There are likely steps you can take right now, even without every tool in place. Focus on what you can do in the meantime and actively work toward securing the technology you need to get the job done.

Each of these resources—time, finances, experts, physical space, technology—plays a critical role in preparing for the work ahead. They help make your transformation smoother and more effective. Depending on your unique journey, there may be additional resources worth identifying and considering to support your path forward.

COMMUNICATION

As you prepare to implement your Path Forward, are there people you need to communicate with? Are there people who you are going to look to for support? Are there people whose lives are going to be impacted? As you start prioritizing differently and making different decisions, are there people who are going to be taken by surprise?

Think about the people in your life you want to share your North Star with—or even just your goals or certain actions. I have never communicated my entire North Star to anyone, but they are certainly seeing it come to fruition. I did share aspects of it with my husband. Other aspects I shared with girlfriends. In some cases, I simply said, "I am looking to expand my community engagement." They didn't need to know the why or that it was part of a larger vision.

Think about who should know what and then communicate that as you see fit. I told my son I was entering my Villain Era*. He is a comic book geek, so he got it immediately and never seemed surprised by any of the changes I was making in my life. In fact, he seemed pretty proud of it and was the least threatened. I got the most high-fives from him.

*Villain Era does not mean that you are turning into a bad guy. It simply means you decide to prioritize yourself.

IMPLEMENTING THE PATH FORWARD

"Knowledge is not power; Implementation is power."
Garrison Wynn

You are ready to work. You have your plan. Follow it. When you Illustrated Your Path Forward, you identified the actions and tools needed to close the gap. You may have created a chart outlining your actions, or you may have built the staircase from the top down, including goals, objectives, strategies, and tactics. Or you may have devised your own way to create your roadmap. Whichever method you chose, now is the time to follow that plan.

TAKE DETERMINED ACTIONS

In Illustrate Your Path Forward, you developed detailed plans to reach your North Star. Now is the time to take those actions.

- *What thoughts are you reframing?*
- *What stories are you cultivating?*
- *What knowledge are you building?*
- *What skills are you developing?*
- *What behaviors, habits, and routines are you releasing and/or adopting?*
- *What symbols or artifacts are you acquiring?*
- *What social environment and support systems are you fostering?*
- *How are you ensuring your physical space is aligned with your vision?*
- *What communities are you building?*
- *Are you surrounding yourself with things that are in alignment with and supportive of your vision?*

NAVIGATING HAZARDS

In Illustrate Your Path Forward, you planned for inevitable hazards and how you would navigate them. Some would be internal, and others would be external. *What expected hazards have shown up? Have you had more internal hazards or external hazards? Have you used your planned strategies for navigating around them? Did those strategies work? If not, did you develop new strategies?*

What have you learned from them that can help you along the remainder of your journey? Remember, hazards can offer new perspectives and valuable lessons. *How have they further informed your journey?*

The important thing as you Forge Ahead is to learn to recognize the hazards, assess them, navigate around them while staying on the trajectory to the North Star, and learn lessons from them.

LEVERAGING ENABLERS

In Illustrate Your Path Forward, you identified enablers—factors that support and accelerate your journey, making change easier to implement. Now, reflect on how those enablers are working for you. *Have you been able to leverage them? How are they showing up in your journey? Have any new or unexpected enablers emerged along the way? What have you learned from them, and how might they shape your understanding of other potential enablers?*

MONITORING & STAYING ON COURSE

In Illustrate Your Path Forward, you identified how to stay on course and remain motivated using mile markers, refueling stations, checkpoints, and scenic views. Now is the time to put those tools into action. Be intentional about when and how you use them. They are essential for sustaining your momentum and measuring your progress. Let's take a moment to revisit each one.

USE YOUR MILE MARKERS TO MONITOR YOUR PROGRESS

How did you decide to define and measure success? What mile markers did you establish? Are you watching out for them along the journey? Based on your mile markers, are you still on course to your North Star, or have you veered off course? Are the goals, objectives, strategies, and tactics working as you expected? Do you need to make adjustments?

"When it is obvious that your goals cannot be reached, don't adjust the goals, adjust the action steps."
Confucius

It is perfectly normal—and you planned for the fact—that your strategies would need to be adjusted along the way. But you don't know that unless you are monitoring your progress, and that is what your mile markers are designed to help you do. Use your mile markers to help determine if you are on the right trajectory, or, alternatively, if you need to make adjustments. If there are no adjustments to be made, you are likely not effectively monitoring your progress.

USE YOUR FUELING AND CHARGING STATIONS TO REFUEL AND ENERGIZE

Put your fueling stations into action. You will need them. Don't ignore them. You may have one form of fueling station or multiple forms. You may refuel daily, weekly, monthly, or quarterly. The important thing is to identify and use the fueling stations.

While in graduate school, I only had two forms of refueling. One was daily, and the other was quarterly. I don't do well without 6 hours of good solid sleep. If I am not sleeping 6 hours, I am not functioning at my best. My daily refueling was stopping whatever I was working on by 9:30pm, spending 30 minutes on a nightly bedtime routine, and closing my eyes by 10:00pm. The 30-minute nighttime routine calmed my nervous system, quieted my brain, and allowed me to sleep.

My other refueling station was built into my calendar quarterly. It was free weekends from Friday at 5:00pm through Sunday at bedtime when absolutely nothing could be put on the calendar. No event, concert, or gathering, not even a movie or a phone call. I was free to use that time anyway I felt like at that moment in time. I could binge-watch TV guilt-free. I could curl up in a chair and read a novel alllll day. I could take a leisurely stroll in the park or clean out a junk drawer. It didn't matter. The point was that for those 48 hours I was completely unencumbered, and for me, that was relaxing and energizing.

What are your refueling stations, and are you putting them to use?

USE YOUR CHECKPOINTS FOR ACCOUNTABILITY

Did you get your accountability buddy? A person or people to keep you accountable? Are you meeting or talking with them at regular intervals? Are you sharing progress updates, hazards you've encountered, and wins you've made?

I had one accountability buddy who, if she did not see a blog post from me every two weeks, was on my phone offering topics for me to consider. She would not let me off the phone until I had chosen a topic and told her the date it would be published. My dissertation editor acted as an accountability buddy. She said when we started working together that I could send her my target dates for each chapter, and she would regularly check my progress in advance of the date. Or if I did not want that accountability help, I did not need to send her my target dates, and she would just get the chapters when she got them. I chose the first option, and sure enough, I'd get gentle nudges that she was looking forward to reading my chapter in a couple of weeks.

But keep in mind it is a mutual relationship. You have to ask them to hold you accountable, and you need to be accountable. If you aren't accountable, the relationship will not work. My North Star included being a golfer, so I could go out with my new girlfriends who golf and join my husband for a day of golfing while we vacation. Don't judge me. I told you at the very beginning that my North Star was all-encompassing. I did not exaggerate. Anyway…

I hired a golf instructor for private lessons once a week. He would also see me at the driving range on the one or two days I practiced on my own. Firstly, I felt bad because although I was working with him once a week, I was not going to the driving range on my own—of which he was fully aware because he was there daily. He mentioned it a few times during our lessons. One week I canceled a lesson. The next week I was out of town, so I canceled that lesson too. Suffice it to say, I ghosted him, and I have not yet become a golfer. Lesson? Don't ghost your accountability buddy and still expect to meet your goals.

USE YOUR SCENIC VIEWS TO CELEBRATE

How are you rewarding yourself along your journey? You get to define your own celebrations. Big wins call for big celebrations, and little wins with little celebrations carry you to the big ones. Choose both. I threw big birthday parties for myself only on my 30th, 40th, and 50th. All the years in between, were small or no parties. But I told my husband one year before I completed my doctoral degree that I wanted him to plan a big graduation party. Big win—big celebration. But to get me there, I gave myself small rewards along the way.

I wrote them out in advance, as I suggested you do in Step 3: Illustrate Your Path Forward. Don't leave them to chance – they won't happen if you do. Scenic views should be plotted on your Path Forward, and you should know how you are going to celebrate. Some of mine included: A new plant, a Sunday morning trip to a local farmers market, a scented candle, a standalone foot or hand massage, a beautiful scented hand fan, a casual stroll around a local bookstore, a bubble bath, leisurely preparing a nice meal while sipping a glass of wine and listening to good music, and a dinner of cheese, crackers, chocolate, and wine.

These were little things, but they were the perfect rewards for me. And they aligned with my focus, which was reconnecting with and prioritizing myself. I didn't need other people to reward me or celebrate with me. These were my celebrations. Yours will be different. Yours will be uniquely you. Yours might be loud and festive. Yours might be shared with people or pets. Just don't hesitate to celebrate!

REFINE YOUR STRATEGY

Refining your strategy during a journey is essential for achieving success. Refining your strategy helps you stay aligned with your ultimate goal, allowing you to adjust short-term strategies without losing sight of the big-picture goal.

Your North Star should remain steadfast. Your strategies for getting there will not. With the information collected as part of your ongoing assessment of progress and reflections, and the lessons learned during implementation, you will know if strategies need to be refined.

Challenges and setbacks are inevitable on any journey. No journey follows a perfectly predictable path. External factors and unforeseen obstacles will arise. Refining your strategy along the way allows you to pivot in response to these uncertainties, ensuring you stay on track toward your goals. Being willing and able to refine the strategy makes it easier to adapt when things don't go as planned and enables you to overcome obstacles without derailing progress. Refining your strategy during the journey prevents stagnation, encouraging continuous evaluation and adjustment for sustained progress.

As you progress through a journey, new insights and knowledge emerge. Refining your strategy allows you to incorporate these learnings and adjust your approach.

REFLECT ON YOUR JOURNEY

"You don't learn from experience; you learn from reflecting on experiences."
John Dewey

Reflection is a vital part of any journey. It allows you to learn, adapt, make informed decisions, celebrate progress, grow, and stay aligned with your North Star. Without it, experiences remain events that happen rather than lessons that shape and guide us.

Philosopher and psychologist John Dewey famously stated, "We don't learn from experience; we learn from reflecting on experience." His words emphasize that true understanding comes not from simply living through something, but from deeply processing it—analyzing, evaluating, and making meaning of what has happened. Transformation doesn't occur by chance; it requires active reflection to turn experiences into insights and insights into action.

Taking time to reflect creates clarity by helping you step back from daily demands and see the bigger picture—where you are, where you've been, and where you're going. It offers an opportunity to assess progress, identify patterns, and determine whether adjustments are needed to stay aligned with your goals.

Reflection also ensures that your journey remains authentic and values-driven. In the midst of long or complex pursuits, it's easy to lose sight of what truly matters. By pausing to reflect, you reinforce alignment between your actions and your values, maintaining integrity and intentionality.

Beyond analyzing success and failure, reflection enhances emotional awareness. It helps you recognize how certain situations made you feel and how those emotions influenced your choices. This self-awareness is key to moving from reactivity to intentionality, allowing you to make decisions with purpose rather than from habit.

Ultimately, reflection transforms experience into wisdom. It is the bridge between what happens and what we learn, ensuring that every step of the journey—whether smooth or challenging—contributes to meaningful growth.

For this reason, intentionally incorporating mirrors into your Path Forward is essential. Regular self-assessment and reflection act as those mirrors, offering valuable feedback to refine your journey and reinforce your commitment to transformation.

CHECK YOUR MIRRORS

Just as you regularly check your mirrors while driving, reflection is an ongoing process. It is not a one-time event or something reserved only for major milestones or mile markers. Reflection should be an active and regular practice during your journey. Mirrors represent ongoing reflection and symbolize regular introspection and self-assessment. They offer moments to pause, realign with your purpose, reflect on lessons learned and gain clarity on your journey.

Without regular reflection, it's easy to become complacent, falling into patterns or routines that may no longer serve you. Ongoing reflection is about self-questioning: *Am I still aligned with my goals? Are my actions moving me forward? Are my actions or inactions holding me back?* It keeps you engaged in intentional progress rather than passively going through the motions.

The more frequently you check your mirrors, the more attuned you become to your thoughts, emotions, and behaviors. This deepens your self-awareness, helping you recognize patterns over time, identifying blind spots, strengths, and areas for growth. Ongoing reflection ensures that you remain aligned and on track to your North Star. In the hustle of daily life or during long-term transformation, it's easy to lose sight of what truly matters and stay connected with your why. Regular reflection helps realign actions and decisions with both your values and goals, ensuring you stay on the path you've consciously chosen.

What prompts you to reflect? Consider the tools and methods that facilitate your reflection process. *Do you have a specific way of capturing your thoughts? To* incorporate reflection into your routine, allocate dedicated time each day or week. You might block time on your calendar or keep a journal beside your bed or in your office. A dedicated journal serves as both a reminder and a space for reflection.

To make your reflections more structured, consider using standard questions that you can ask yourself regularly. Additionally, create a ritual by integrating reflection into existing routines, such as your morning coffee or nightly bedtime routine. By employing techniques that remind you to reflect, you can cultivate a sustainable reflection practice that supports your ongoing transformation.

A DYNAMIC INTERPLAY

Forging Ahead involves a dynamic interplay between action, monitoring, adjustments, and reflection. The steps you take to pursue your North Star, the way you monitor your progress, the adjustments you make to stay on course, and your reflections throughout the journey are all interconnected, working in harmony to foster continuous development.

These elements interact, inform, and influence one another, creating a mutual exchange that enhances overall progress. Rather than occurring in a linear sequence, they operate in a cyclical manner, moving in parallel and in tandem, with each supporting the others in an ongoing evolution. This relationship ensures that each component drives and sustains the forward motion of the entire transformation.

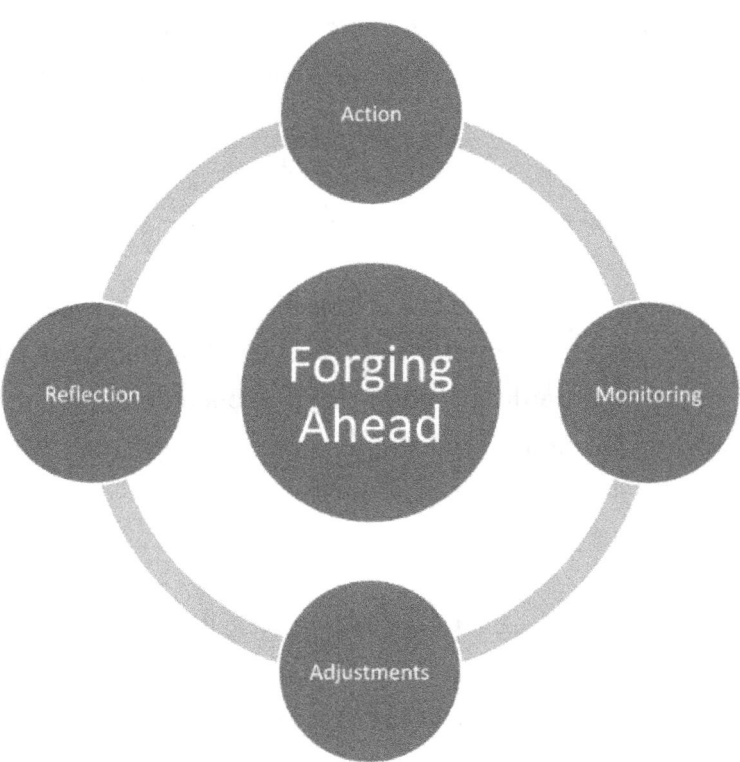

ANCHOR POINT

At this stage in your SHIFT journey, you've transitioned from visioning to doing. You are no longer just imagining transformation—you're embodying it. The planning is behind you, and purposeful action is underway. You are navigating real-world obstacles, recognizing wins, and making adjustments in real time. This is the active phase—where momentum builds and movement toward your North Star becomes visible and tangible.

The keys to sustained transformation are intentional action, continuous reflection, and strategic adaptation. As you navigate this journey, keep checking your mile markers, leveraging your enablers, and staying vigilant for hazards. Remember, the Path Forward is not linear; it is dynamic. There will be detours, slowdowns, and moments when you need to recalibrate. That is part of the process.

Stay present. Stay committed. Stay reflective. Use your fueling stations to recharge, your checkpoints for accountability, and your scenic views to celebrate your wins—big and small. The momentum you build now will carry you forward, making your transformation not just an idea, but a reality.

As you transition into Step 5: Thrive Unapologetically, you will deepen your alignment with your North Star and develop the resilience needed to sustain long-term transformation. You are already on your way—keep moving.

FOLLOW MY JOURNEY

As Michelle Obama says, you have to practice every day who you want to be. There are some aspects of my North Star that are accomplishments and others that are daily practices.

In my North Star, I am Dr. Nicole Yeldell Butts. One aspect of that is an accomplishment. I earned a doctorate degree. I have it. Accomplishment complete. But also in my North Star, I am an attentive daughter, daughter-in-law, mother, sister, and friend. That is not something I accomplish and check off the list. It is something I have to practice daily.

Creating dedicated space for myself is something I can accomplish but using it to support and value myself is a daily practice. I can go out and buy plants for my home in one morning, but caring for them and ensuring they thrive has become part of my regular routine. The practice of watering and talking to them is one way I honor myself as I pause, shut out the external noise, and enjoy the peace I have created around me. Walking past them and noticing them growing new leaves, stretching out, and reaching up gives me joy.

Can I earn a doctorate while running a consulting business, working full-time, writing books, and doing TEDx Talks? Well, maybe someone else could, but I didn't. My consulting business disappeared, no books got written, and no TEDx Talks were done while I went to school and worked full-time. Does that mean that my business, books, and TEDx Talks are an unreasonable part of my North Star? Absolutely not. It just means I am still navigating to my North Star.

I utilize my allocated resources. In terms of time, I allocate time for the things I am trying to achieve. I create and use daily, weekly, and monthly schedules that break my day and days into focus areas. I put things on my calendar so that time is blocked out. For me, if it is not on my calendar, it does not exist. I allocated money for certain things. For me, financial resources are often tied to experts. For instance, I built an editor into my dissertation process. I focused on the research and content while I had the editor focus on APA formatting. I allocated dedicated space in my house for an office so I could have a quiet place to work, and when I was in my office, people knew not to disturb me.

I have and will continue to encounter roadblocks, most anticipated and some unanticipated. Most are internal roadblocks. One of my biggest roadblocks is the bed. It is so comfy and warm, there are mornings I simply want to stay in it and dream. Another roadblock— and one I did not anticipate because it had never been a problem for me in the past—is social media. In particular, TikTok. I can get lost in dog videos for wayyyyy too long.

I leverage my enablers daily and discover new enablers, mostly in the form of technology that I did not know existed or did not know how to use.

I discovered something new about me and my fueling stations: I *need to recharge before I feel depleted. If I wait until I'm visibly tired or emotionally drained, it's already too late. Proactive renewal—rather than reactive recovery—is what keeps me steady. When I ignore the signs and push through, I eventually crash, and that's when the bingeing begins—on snacks, on TV, on anything that offers a quick hit of comfort.*

There's a funny thread on social media about how men who are with Type A women need to step in and say, "Hey babe… you're spiraling. Go take a nap. I'll handle things." And honestly? That's the energy I need from myself. I need to be the one who notices the signs early, steps in, and says: Pause. Rest. Reset. Not because I'm failing, but because I'm worth sustaining.

I check my mirrors regularly in the form of morning meditation and journaling, and also the occasional evening journaling. I find that checking my mirrors keeps me aligned, committed, motivated, and adaptable.

THRIVE UNAPOLOGETICALLY

"Now that we are no longer striving to survive, let us thrive – and do so without justification or apology."
Nicole Yeldell Butts

When you've spent so long striving, it can feel unfamiliar—almost uncomfortable—to just be. But this is part of the transformation too: the ability to pause, breathe, and live in your becoming without explanation, justification or apology.

In this final step, you'll take stock not from lack, but from love. You'll honor the commitment you've made to yourself and reflect on how far you've come—not just in actions, but in alignment. You'll acknowledge the ways you've begun to live fully in your becoming—

showing up more truthfully, boldly, and unapologetically. And with intention, you'll ask: *Now that I'm here, what does thriving look like for me, and where am I being called to reach for more?*

Full disclosure: I have two favorite steps in this framework. The first step and the last step. Setting Your North Star is one of my favorites because it allows us to envision the future, and I love envisioning the future. Thrive Unapologetically is also a favorite because it reminds us and allows us to live in the vision we created. It grants us permission to rejoice, to honor ourselves, to be in alignment and peace. It encourages us to reflect on our road to achieving our vision, and it encourages us to also consider what is next. So in Thrive Unapologetically, I get to both reflect and continue visioning. I am most certainly in my happy place. So with that transparency, allow me to welcome you to the final step of SHIFT— Thrive Unapologetically.

I said at the beginning that transformation is a journey. In Step 1, you started your journey with the end in mind by Setting Your North Star. In Step 2, you determined where you currently are in relation to that North Star by identifying your Here. In Step 3, you designed a roadmap to close the gap between your North Star and your Here by Illustrating your Path Forward. In step 4, Forge Ahead, you got to work implementing that plan. Step 5: Thrive Unapologetically is about being in alignment with who you always envisioned yourself to be, while continuing to explore more of yourself.

You've done the hard work. You've clarified your North Star, gotten honest about your starting point, envisioned your future, and taken bold, aligned action. Now, it's time to allow yourself to live in the fullness of what you've created.

From here, you will:

- Commit to yourself
- Live fully in your becoming
- Keep reaching, keep rising

COMMIT TO YOURSELF

"The most courageous act is to show up for yourself over and over again
-especially when the world has taught you not to."
Nicole Yeldell Butts

By the end of the first chapter in this book, I had shared with you two personal encounters of self-abandonment. My greatest life lessons have come from the realization of self-abandonment. Learning what it is. Its impact. Learning to recognize when and how it is happening. Unlearning it and learning how to commit to myself.

What does it mean to commit to yourself? And how do you do it?

The good news is that you have already started the process. In Step 1 you defined who you want to be and how you want to show up in the world; for yourself and for others. You identified internal barriers to showing up in the fullness of who you are. In step 2 you uncovered some of the ways you have abandoned yourself in the form of foundational and limiting beliefs, the stories you tell yourself, and some habits and conditioning. In step 3 you devised a strategy to overcome many of these things. You are well on your way to understanding when and how you may have shrunk or abandoned yourself.

You are now better equipped to recognize why, when and how you have a tendency to shrink. With this knowledge, you can now consciously and courageously commit to yourself.

What do I mean when I say commit to yourself? I mean choosing yourself. Showing up for yourself. Making self-honoring choices; choices that honor the person you are and are choosing to become. It is being present for yourself, just like you are present for other people. It is not putting yourself and your needs after something or someone else.

It is also about realizing that the only person who has an obligation to you is you. No one else has an obligation to ensure your well-being—emotionally, physically, mentally, spiritually. If you want to be well, you have to take the steps to be well. There is no knight in shining armor. You are no damsel in distress. You are a fully functioning, fully capable, whole complete person who is responsible for showing up fully for you.

This is not intended to sound lonely, sad, jaded, or cynical. It is in fact none of those things. What it is is true and if you allow it to be, it is empowering and freeing. Instead of looking around outside of yourself for someone else to do for you, take care of you, ensure your well-being, you can step in the place of knowing that no matter what happens with anyone else, you are going to thrive because you are enough, and you will always show up for you. You will not drop her off at the doorstep, hoping a nice family will take you in.

Choosing not to abandon yourself doesn't mean you have to go it alone. You absolutely can—and should—have people in your life who support you. People you can rely on through both the highs and the lows. A partner who lifts you up. Friends who hold you down. Relationships rooted in trust, care, and mutual presence.

Not abandoning yourself and having people you can rely on are not mutually exclusive.

Not abandoning yourself doesn't make you hard, unapproachable, or isolated. It means you are deeply committed to your own vision and values. It means you trust yourself to make decisions that honor who you are—and who you are becoming. It means you show up for yourself first, so you can receive support from others without losing your center.

Thriving isn't just about what you do—it's about who you choose to be, again and again.

And thriving unapologetically means you stop negotiating your becoming.

Thriving unapologetically means:
You are not abandoning yourself anymore.
Not for approval.
Not for tradition.
Not for comfort.
Not for the version of you that makes others feel safe.

Committing to yourself is sacred work. It's the promise you make— not to stay the same, but to stay true.
True to your values.
True to your boundaries.
True to the woman you are becoming.

It means choosing alignment over expectation. Growth over performance. Peace over perfection.

This kind of commitment requires more than intention—it requires practice. It shows up in how you spend your time, how you speak to yourself, what you say yes and no to, and whether you honor the life you say you want.

To thrive unapologetically, you must stop treating your needs, desires, and well-being like they're optional. You stop diminishing your worth. You stop shrinking just to stay connected to places and people you've outgrown.

Commitment to yourself is not a one-time decision—it's a daily devotion.

And the more consistently you show up for you, the more your life begins to reflect the fullness of who you truly are.

SELF-ADVOCACY

Thriving unapologetically and committing to yourself requires more than confidence—it demands *consciousness* and *courage*. One of the most powerful, and often overlooked, expressions of both is self-advocacy.

To thrive, you must recognize and commit to your worth—and be willing to speak and act in alignment with it.

Too many of us were raised to believe that advocating for ourselves is selfish, aggressive, or unbecoming. We were taught to be agreeable, to minimize our needs, and to wait for recognition or permission. But thriving isn't about staying silent or hoping someone else sees your value. It's about owning your voice. It's about standing rooted in your truth—even when it shakes the ground beneath you.

Self-advocacy is the ability to identify and articulate your needs, desires, boundaries, and rights—and to do so with clarity, conviction, and respect. It means asking for what you need without apology. It means protecting your time, your energy, your voice, and your vision. It means honoring your own humanity as much as you've honored everyone else's.

WHY THRIVING REQUIRES SELF ADVOCACY

You cannot thrive in silence. You cannot thrive while being overlooked, overworked, or over-accommodating. Thriving unapologetically means living in alignment with your truth—not shrinking to maintain the comfort of others or waiting for someone to give you what you've already earned.

Self-advocacy is not arrogance—it's alignment.
It's not confrontation—it's clarity.
It's not selfishness—it's self-honoring.

When you advocate for yourself, you send a message—to your body, your spirit, and the world—that your needs matter. That your boundaries are sacred. That your presence is not negotiable.

You may need to advocate for yourself when:
- Your contributions are being minimized or ignored
- Your time is being consumed without respect or

reciprocity

- Your boundaries are being violated, pushed, or dismissed
- Your voice is not being heard, welcomed, or valued
- Your needs, health, or well-being are consistently deprioritized
- You feel yourself disappearing in service to others' comfort

If you've ever walked away from a conversation replaying what you should have said... or swallowed your needs to keep the peace... that was a moment for self-advocacy. And those moments can become turning points.

Self-advocacy is a muscle. It builds over time, with use and intention. Here's how you begin:

Know What You Need: Start by getting clear. What do you actually want? What would support you in this moment? Clarity is the foundation of advocacy.

Give Yourself Permission: You do not need to earn the right to speak up. You don't need a crisis to justify your needs. You are allowed to take up space, ask for support, or set a limit simply because you are worthy.

Communicate Clearly and Calmly: Use "I" statements. Be direct but grounded. Example: "I need more time to complete this project at the quality I'm committed to." or "I'm not available for that right now."

Practice Ahead of Time: Rehearse the words. Write them down. Say them out loud. Advocacy gets easier when it's no longer a surprise to your own nervous system.

Hold the Line with Grace: Boundaries are not walls—they are doors with locks. You decide what and who gets access. And you don't owe guilt, explanation, or performance to keep your boundaries in place.

Stay Rooted in Truth: Your truth may disrupt someone else's comfort. That doesn't make it any less true. You're not here to be palatable—you're here to be whole.

Advocating for yourself is not about fighting to be seen. It's about remembering that you already are.

You are the author of your life—not just the supporting character in someone else's. And when you advocate for yourself, you become the loudest, clearest advocate for your own thriving.

So ask for the raise.
Say no to the obligation.
Request the time you need.
Speak your truth in the meeting.

Name the thing that's been unspoken for too long.

Because you're not here to *survive silently.*
You're here to *thrive unapologetically.*

LIVE FULLY IN YOUR BECOMING

"For me, becoming isn't a goal. It's a process. A way of living."
Michel'e Obama

Why is this section entitled, Live Fully in Your Becoming instead of Live Fully in Who You Have Become? Because one thing I hope you have discovered along this journey is that there is no final "become". You are always Becoming. Michelle Obama spoke this perfectly in her memoir *Becoming*.

"Becoming isn't about arriving somewhere or achieving a certain aim. I see it instead as forward motion, a means of evolving, a way to reach continuously toward a better self. The journey doesn't end."

Thriving isn't just about what you do—it's about who you choose to be, again and again.

And thriving *unapologetically* means you stop negotiating your becoming. And now, with your personal North Star set, your becoming can always align with your guiding compass.

Thriving Unapologetically is a recognition and affirmation that growth is continuous, deeply personal, and about alignment, not perfection. You've done the deep work. Now it's time to stand in it— fully. Thriving unapologetically isn't passive; it's a conscious, courageous choice to live in alignment with who you are becoming. To stay awake to your joy, your truth, and your freedom.

How do you root into that thriving space with intention?

SELF-RECOGNIZE

Return to the questions you asked yourself earlier in your SHIFT journey—but this time, ask them through a new lens: *How have I grown since I began to Forge Ahead? What patterns have shifted? What moments tested me, and how did I show up?*

You're not looking for perfection—you're looking for evolution. Let your mirror moments (from Forge Ahead) guide you in celebrating your resilience, honesty, and alignment. When you see where you've shown up differently, own it. That's thriving.

Yes, reflection still matters. In fact, Thriving Unapologetically means celebrating your progress with as much intentionality as you once used to assess your gaps.

Remember your baseline Here from Step 2? That was your starting point—your raw, honest, truth. It helped you see clearly what needed to change. Today, it helps you see clearly how far you've come.

Revisit it, not to critique, but to witness your evolution. Measure your growth not just by what's changed externally, but by how you feel internally—more aligned, more empowered, more you.

You can still use the tools of reflection and accountability—your checkpoints and mirrors—but now they're affirming tools, not correcting ones. Let them remind you of what's working. Let them show you how transformation is taking root.

Thriving Unapologetically means giving yourself permission to enjoy this version of you—without guilt, hesitation, or shrinking. You are not who you were. You are who you've chosen to become.

I'll never forget a moment with one of my coaching clients—a high-achieving executive who had spent decades chasing titles, milestones, and external validation. When we first began our work together, she could clearly articulate what wasn't working but struggled to name what she wanted beyond achievement. Months later, during one of our final sessions, she said, "For the first time in my adult life, I feel at home in myself." She wasn't climbing a ladder anymore. She wasn't fixing or proving—she was simply living. Joyfully. Confidently. On her terms.

That's what it means to Thrive Unapologetically. Not because everything is perfect. But because you've made peace with the process, claimed your growth, and chosen to delight in your becoming.

NOTICE YOUR SURROUNDINGS

What's different around you—and within you? Your surroundings often reflect your growth before you even name it. Have your surroundings changed? You may have already reflected on this as you have been Forging Ahead. *Have your physical, social, and professional surroundings changed, or the way you engage with them? Has your community engagement changed? What are you taking in now that may be different from what you were taking in before? How are your daily routines reflecting your values and goals? Have your spaces changed? Your relationships? Your energy? Even your routines?*

Notice how you move through the world now. Are your days shaped by your values? Is your life reflecting your North Star in real time? Thriving isn't just about where you are—it's about how you are in it.

INVITE WITNESSING

Reach out to the trusted voices who walked part of this journey with you—those who gave honest feedback when you needed it most. Ask them: *What do you see in me now? What's shifted?*

If you've had an accountability partner, you may already have some of these reflections. But now, this isn't just about course-correcting. It's about letting yourself be seen—not as a work in progress, but as a woman becoming.

KEEP REACHING, KEEP RISING

"The summit is just a halfway point."
Edward Viesturs

You set out on a journey of transformation to get to a place you have not been before. Once we arrive, we have to ask, *Is this what we were reaching for? Is it what you hoped it would be? Is it what you expected it would be? Is it aligned with your values and goals?*

Thriving Unapologetically doesn't mean settling in—it means expanding.

Transformation isn't linear. It doesn't end the moment you hit a goal, receive the promotion, find clarity, or feel whole. In truth, those moments are simply new vantage points—proof of what's possible and invitations to imagine more.

You didn't come all this way to arrive and shrink. You came to rise, rest, and rise again—on your terms.

From this elevated view, you get to ask: What's next? Not out of obligation, but from a place of purpose, freedom, and joy. Do you want to go deeper in this area? Explore something entirely new? Revisit a path you once abandoned but now see through fresh eyes? Set new sights.

Setting new sights isn't about not being satisfied or always needing more.   It's about intentional expansion—growing in alignment with your values, your voice, and your vision. It keeps your evolution alive, your energy flowing, and your life attuned to the truth of who you are now becoming.

Your definition of thriving will change as you do. Let it. Let your goals stretch with you. Let your dreams evolve. Let your joy lead the way.

You are not done. You are just in a new chapter of your unfolding.

DELVE DEEPER: DOING MORE WITH YOUR CURRENT FOCUS AREAS

It is highly likely that during this journey you discovered ways you would like to drill down into your values and goals. Maybe you saw ways you could further embed your values into your life. Maintaining your current North Star, *how might you incorporate it into your life in other ways not yet done?*

Along your path, you may have also noticed that some goals are no longer as aligned with your values as they once were. Consider revisiting and refining them. Perhaps a career milestone you once aimed for now seems less fulfilling, and a shift towards a more purpose-driven goal feels more appropriate. The key is maintaining clarity on how your goals reflect the deeper values you hold dear.

BROADEN AND EXPAND: ADDING NEW FOCUS AREAS TO YOUR EXISTING NORTH STAR

In Step 2, you identified several focus areas for transformation, but I encouraged you to prioritize 3-5 for the time being. The idea was to concentrate on those key areas, allowing you to address others later, once the initial focus areas had been fully solidified. Now, you may be ready to shift your attention to those additional focus areas.

While your North Star remains steady, you will need to reassess your Here to accommodate these new priorities. You'll need to Illustrate a new Path Forward, one that aligns with your evolving focus areas. The techniques and strategies you used to make progress previously, if they proved effective, will likely continue to serve you well as you navigate this new chapter.

Remember, your North Star can evolve in meaning as your life progresses. Consider how you might expand into areas you haven't yet explored, broadening your journey while staying anchored in your core purpose.

GO BEYOND: DEVELOPING A NEW NORTH STAR

During your journey, you may have encountered something completely new and surprising that now compels you to explore it further. Life has a way of offering unexpected opportunities that both surprise and captivate us. These moments of unexpected revelation can serve as powerful catalysts for future growth and exploration.

I went to Italy eager to see Michelangelo's work but unexpectedly fell in love with Caravaggio's. Similarly, perhaps your journey brought something new into your awareness—something that resonates deeply and invites further exploration. These serendipitous discoveries are reminders to stay open to life's surprises. The key is not only to recognize these unexpected moments but also to embrace them fully, allowing them to guide you toward new and meaningful directions.

Whatever you choose to set as your new sight, remember you have the framework to achieve it. Simply apply the same SHIFT framework to your new sights.

ANCHOR POINT

Transformation is not a destination—it is an ongoing journey.

You've arrived at a powerful moment in your SHIFT journey. You Set Your North Star, assessed your Here, Illustrated Your Path Forward, and Forged Ahead. Now, you stand in a new space—rooted, radiant, and ready to Thrive Unapologetically.

Thriving Unapologetically is about ownership—of your choices, your truth, and your evolution. It's about commitment—not to a role or a goal, but to yourself. Thriving Unapologetically means staying loyal to the woman you are becoming, even when it's uncomfortable, even when it disrupts what others expect of you.

This is your invitation to live fully in your becoming—to embody the vision you've held, to trust the wisdom you've earned, and to take up space without shrinking, second-guessing, or needing permission.

Every journey changes us. Perhaps you feel fully aligned with where you are now. Or maybe the road has revealed new desires, dreams, or directions. Whether you're choosing to deepen this path or explore a new one, one thing is clear: You are the author of what comes next.

- Will you expand what you've built and trust yourself to go even deeper?

- Will you give yourself full permission to express who you are becoming?
- Will you dare to rise again—boldly, bravely, and without apology?

You already have the tools, the clarity, and the courage. You've done more than shift—you've awakened.

This is not the end of your SHIFT—it's the continuation of your boldly becoming.

FOLLOW MY JOURNEY

I used to think thriving would feel like standing in front of the Mona Lisa—arriving at something universally celebrated, something everyone said I should want. And yet, when I finally stood in that crowded room at the Louvre, peering at her through a sea of people, I wasn't moved. What captivated me instead was what was directly opposite her: The Wedding Feast at Cana by Paolo Veronese. I hadn't come to see that painting. I hadn't expected to love it. But it was the one that spoke to my spirit.

Thriving, I've learned, isn't always found where others tell you it should be. It's not always found in the spotlight or the trophy moment. Sometimes it's found where you least expect it—on the opposite wall, in a quiet corner, in the thing you didn't even know to dream about.

Thriving Unapologetically shows up most strongly for me in the form of not abandoning myself. This is particularly true in my business. My life as a solopreneur can be isolating, lonely, scary and often challenges my sense of security. But to abandon my business—the business that is a reflection of who I am, how I show up, what I want to offer the world and the legacy I want to leave behind—would be to abandon myself. So, I have to remind myself, daily, as a solopreneur to not go back to an employer, not to walk away from my business, even when times are hard and I am not sure when the next check is coming in. Thriving Unapologetically means I stand firm, I show up, I believe, I fight. When people in my life use terms like "unemployed" or "not working", I boldly reframe their notions of what it means to work and their base assumption that work means being employed by someone else.

Another place it shows up for me is in my morning routine. I really don't like waking up in the morning and going to the gym. I'd rather stay in bed to cuddle and dream. But going to the gym every morning is a self-honoring act. I honor the fact that I need to keep my physical and emotional energy high and that keeping my body strong and healthy is critical to that.

What has it meant for me to Thrive Unapologetically: To take up my full rightful space. To define success on my own terms. And to live—not just exist—rooted in my own truth no longer explaining, justifying, negotiating, or apologizing for it. It's been like learning how to simply say "Thank You" when given a compliment and unlearning the instinct to say, "oh no, it really wasn't anything special."

For me, thriving without explanation, justification or apology is like living in my favorite quote.

"For the self is a sea boundless and measureless... The soul unfolds itself, like a lotus of countless petals."
Kahlil Gibran

I am boundless, measureless, infinite. I am constantly unfolding, expanding, growing, learning, and experiencing. That is why I am here. To live a full, beautiful, complex life. I am always discovering more of who I am, can be and want to be. That is my right, my privilege and my joy. No one can take it from me, and I live into it. That for me is what Thriving Unapologetically is.

FINAL THOUGHTS

As we come to the end of this book, I hope you feel empowered, inspired, and ready to embark on your own journey of transformation. This journey requires consciousness and courage— the consciousness to see where you want to go and where you are today, and the courage to take the necessary steps to close the gap between the two.

Transformation is not for the faint of heart. It demands self-reflection, courage, and a commitment to move beyond what is familiar or comfortable. Yet, as I have shared throughout this book, it is also a deeply rewarding process. One that will not only change your external reality but also fill your internal world with a sense of authenticity, fullness, and peace.

This book was written to provide a clear, actionable framework for anyone seeking to navigate personal transformation with intention. Whether you've just started reflecting on the choices you make or you've been working to improve your life for years, this five-point SHIFT framework gives you the tools to take action that aligns with your True North.

To briefly recap:

Set Your North Star: Always begin with the end in mind. This will guide your journey and remind you of your ultimate vision.

Here-You Are Here: Knowing where you're going is only half the equation. You must also determine where you are today—your current reality.

Illustrate Your Path Forward: With your destination and current position in view, create a roadmap to close the gap.

Forge Ahead: Once the path is mapped, take decisive actions toward your goal.

Thrive Unapologetically: Fully embrace your authentic becoming

Along the way, remember the importance of granting yourself grace. As I said earlier, "I make the best choices I can based on who I want to be and the information I have at the time." This is not only a reflection of how I live my life, but also an invitation for you to live yours with the same understanding. You will make choices that feel difficult or imperfect, but with grace, you can trust that each decision is part of your evolution. Regret has no place here because you acted with the best intentions and knowledge available to you at the time.

The only thing required of you now is the desire to transform—to move from where you are today to where you truly want to be. If you have that, the SHIFT framework w ll guide you through the rest.

Thank you for joining me on this journey. I hope this framework will serve you well as you continue to grow and transform. As Buddha reminds us, "Each morning we are born again. What we do today is what matters most."

Here's to your transformation—conscious, courageous, and full of grace.

About the Author

Dr. Nicole Yeldell Butts is a sought-after transformational coach, dynamic speaker, and best-selling author who has made it her mission to help high-achieving women stop playing small and start living unapologetically.

Armed with decades of leadership experience, a doctorate in Organizational Change & Leadership, and her groundbreaking SHIFT Framework, she guides women through intentional, courageous transformation that delivers lasting results.

Known for her bold truth-telling, strategic insight, and deep compassion, Dr. Nicole has helped countless women reclaim their vision, amplify their voice, and create lives that reflect their boldest ambitions.

Based in Los Angeles, she brings her unstoppable energy and wisdom to stages, organizations, and individuals worldwide.

Learn more at https://www.nicolebutts.com